ART LOVE PASSION

Dogs & Doodles
Volume 2

©2015 by Angelika Parker

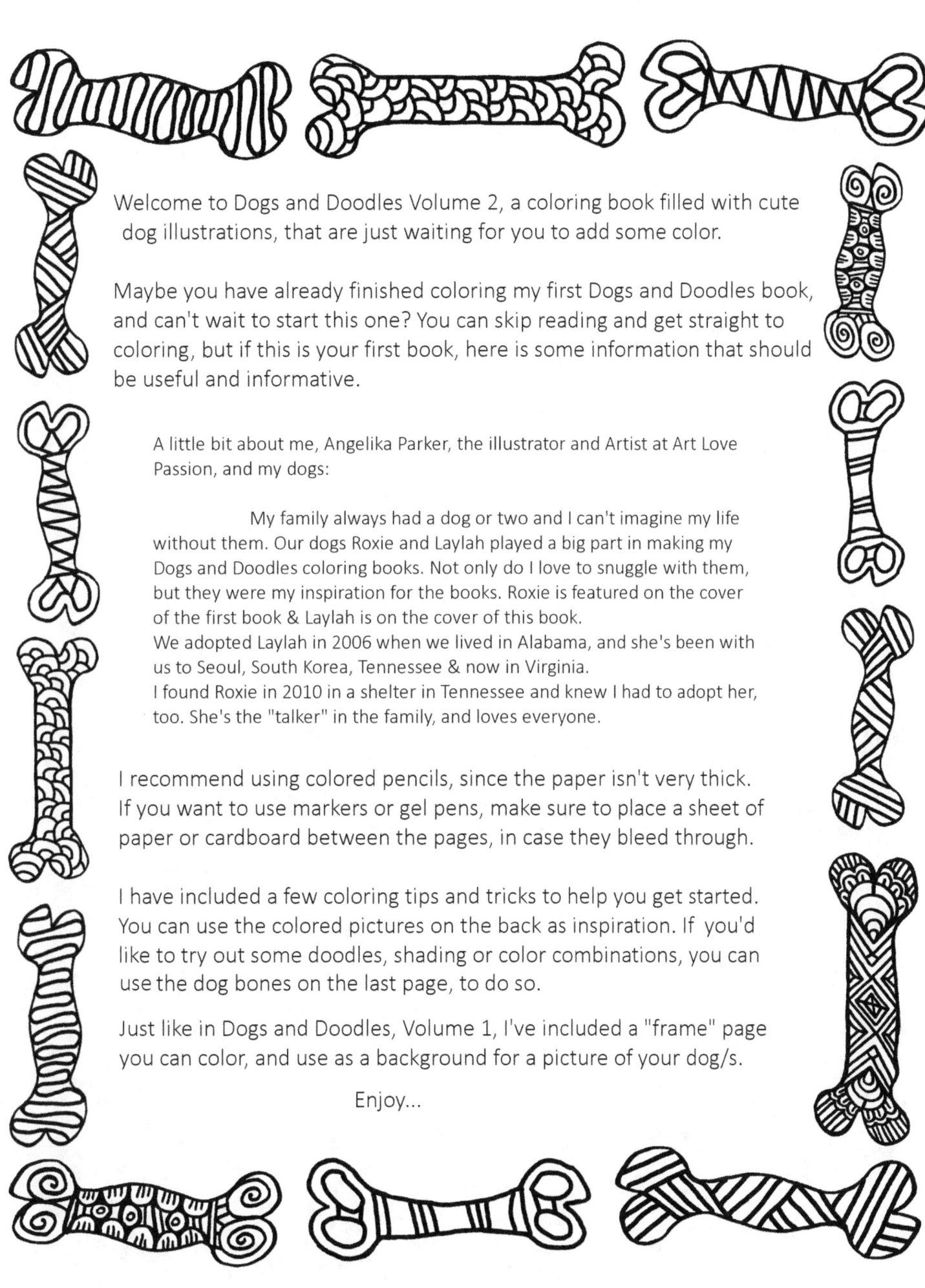

Welcome to Dogs and Doodles Volume 2, a coloring book filled with cute dog illustrations, that are just waiting for you to add some color.

Maybe you have already finished coloring my first Dogs and Doodles book, and can't wait to start this one? You can skip reading and get straight to coloring, but if this is your first book, here is some information that should be useful and informative.

A little bit about me, Angelika Parker, the illustrator and Artist at Art Love Passion, and my dogs:

My family always had a dog or two and I can't imagine my life without them. Our dogs Roxie and Laylah played a big part in making my Dogs and Doodles coloring books. Not only do I love to snuggle with them, but they were my inspiration for the books. Roxie is featured on the cover of the first book & Laylah is on the cover of this book.
We adopted Laylah in 2006 when we lived in Alabama, and she's been with us to Seoul, South Korea, Tennessee & now in Virginia.
I found Roxie in 2010 in a shelter in Tennessee and knew I had to adopt her, too. She's the "talker" in the family, and loves everyone.

I recommend using colored pencils, since the paper isn't very thick. If you want to use markers or gel pens, make sure to place a sheet of paper or cardboard between the pages, in case they bleed through.

I have included a few coloring tips and tricks to help you get started. You can use the colored pictures on the back as inspiration. If you'd like to try out some doodles, shading or color combinations, you can use the dog bones on the last page, to do so.

Just like in Dogs and Doodles, Volume 1, I've included a "frame" page you can color, and use as a background for a picture of your dog/s.

Enjoy...

Coloring Tips & Tricks

Before you begin coloring, test out your colors on some scrap paper. A lot of times the color on a marker looks very different from the color of that same marker on a piece of paper.
The same goes with colored pencils and gel pens. This will give you a better idea of what your finished piece will look like.

Mixing colors with colored pencils is easier when you use multiple layers. Start with a light layer and keep adding more layers, rather then pressing down hard. Finish your piece by using a colorless blender that will fuse the colors together and will make them look more vibrant.

You can also mix mediums. You could start with a marker and go over it with a colored pencil, or vice versa.

For more tips and tricks, check out some videos online.

Don't be afraid to try new things. Use these dog bones for color combinations, shading or for some random doodles you like.

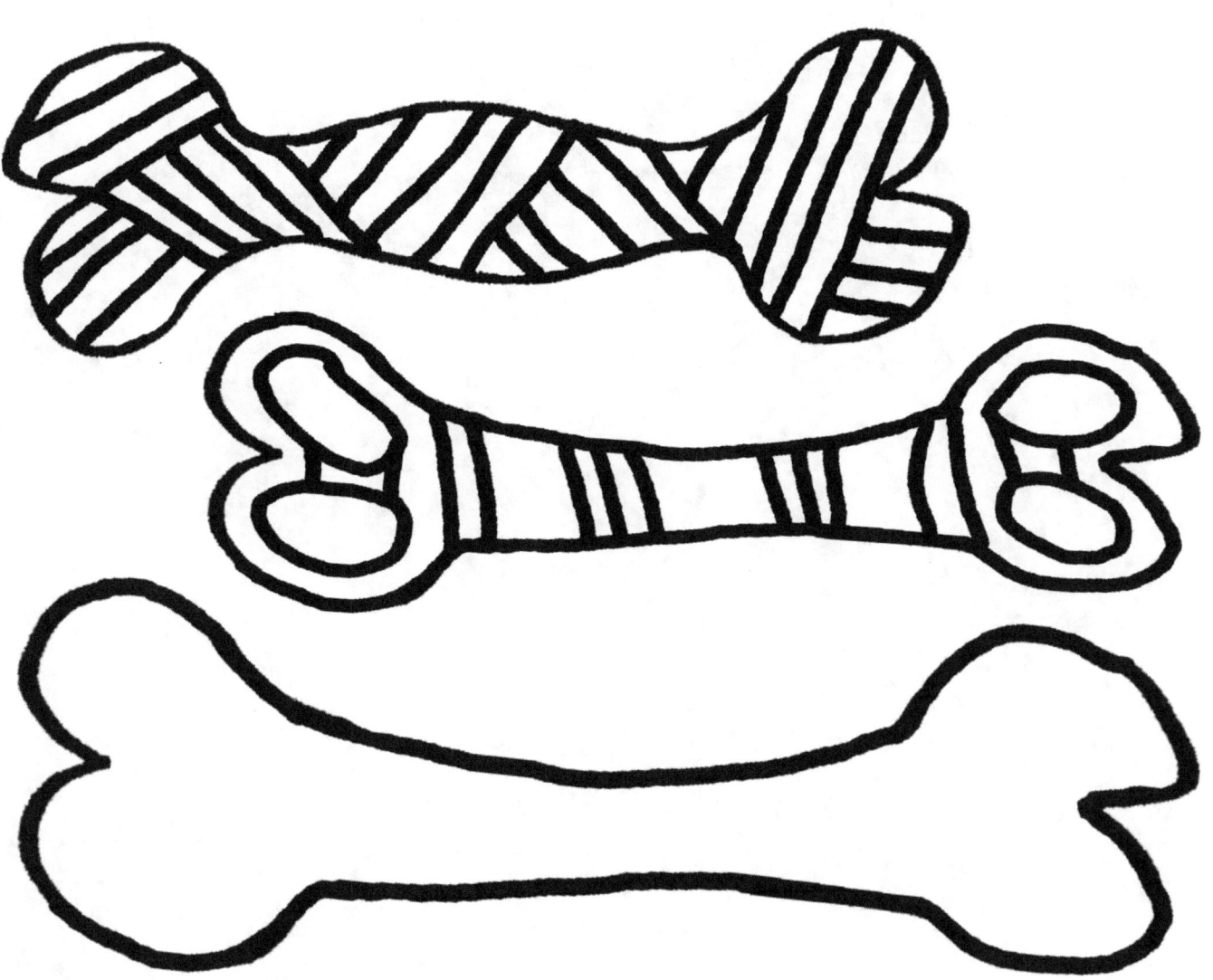

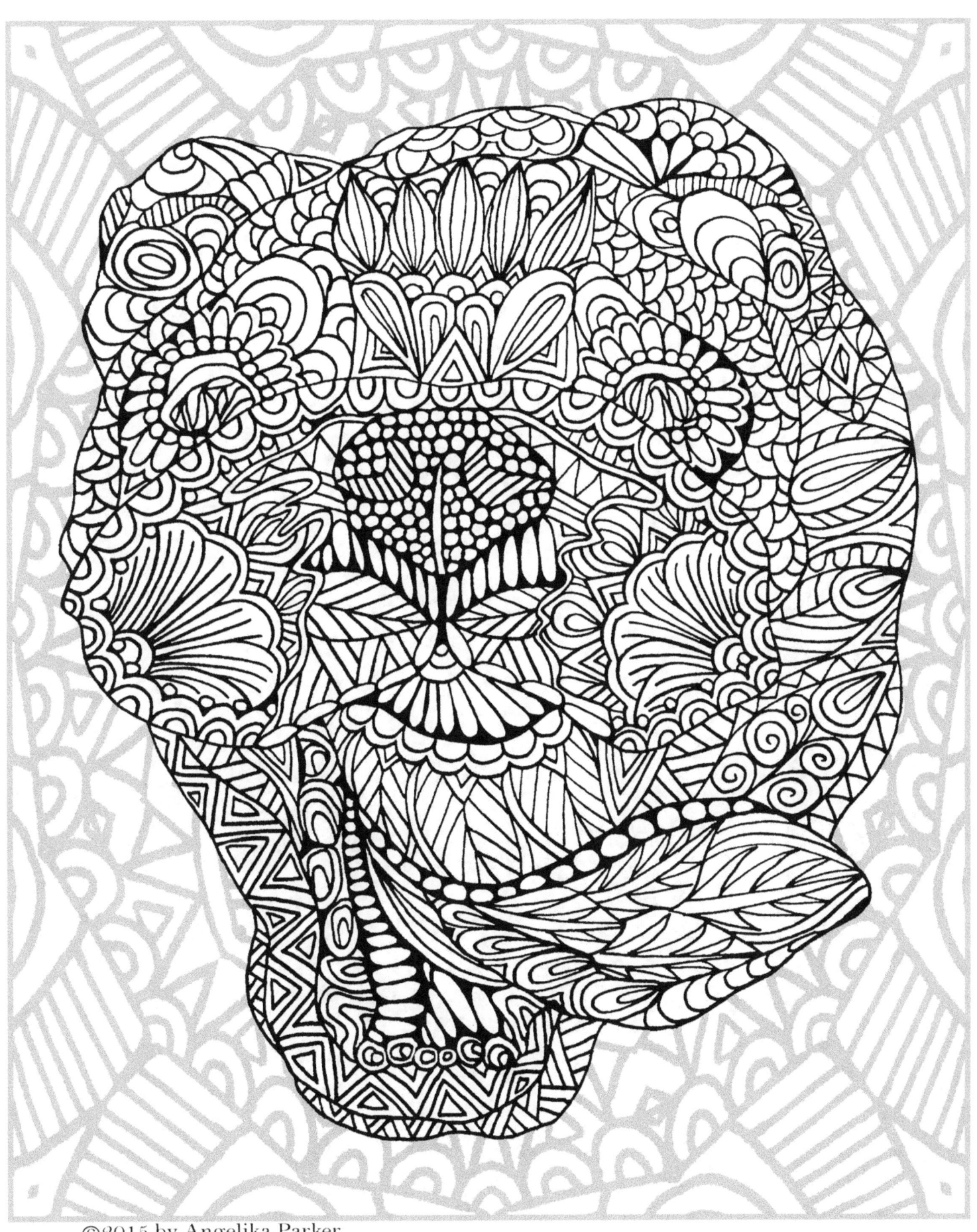

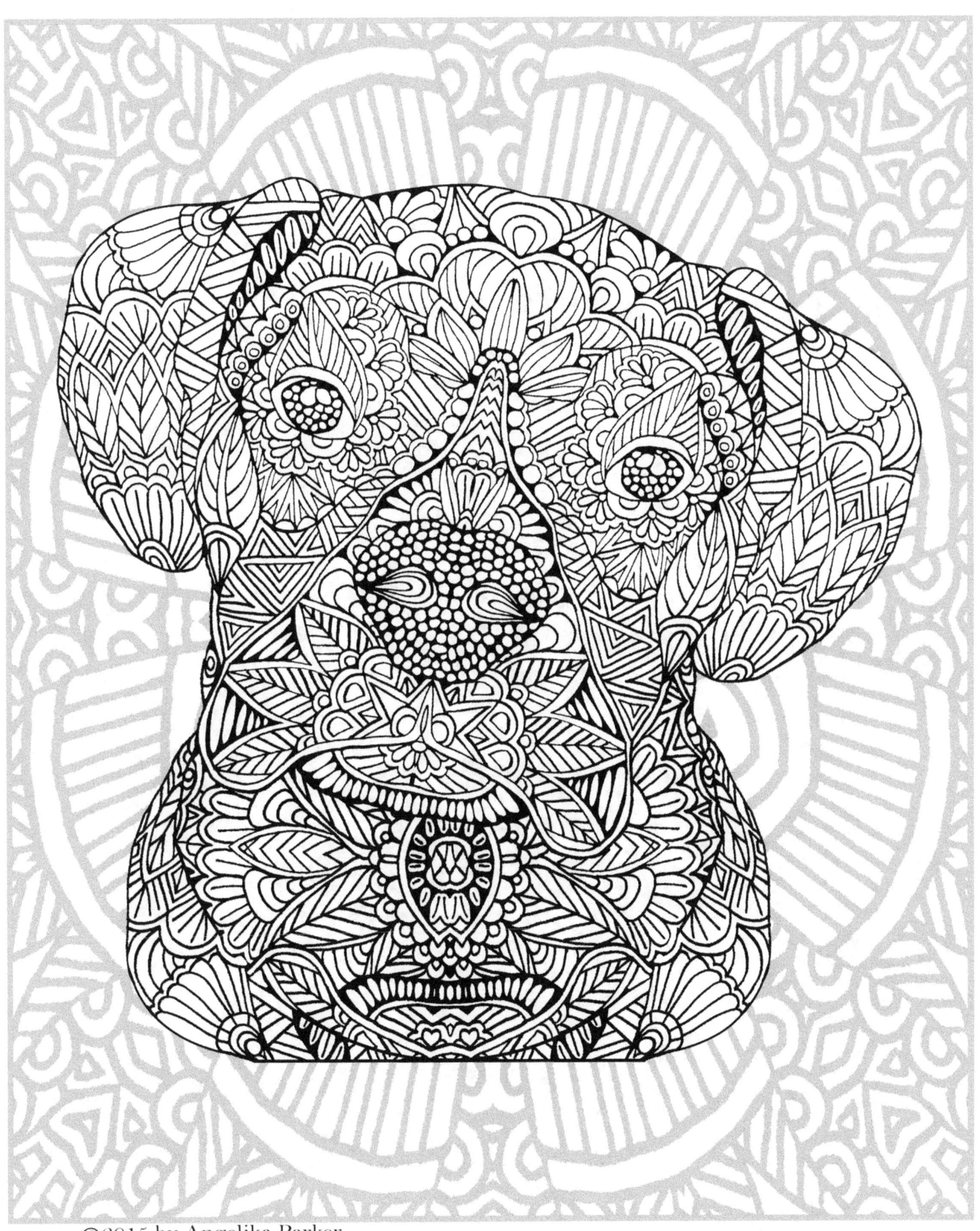

©2015 by Angelika Parker

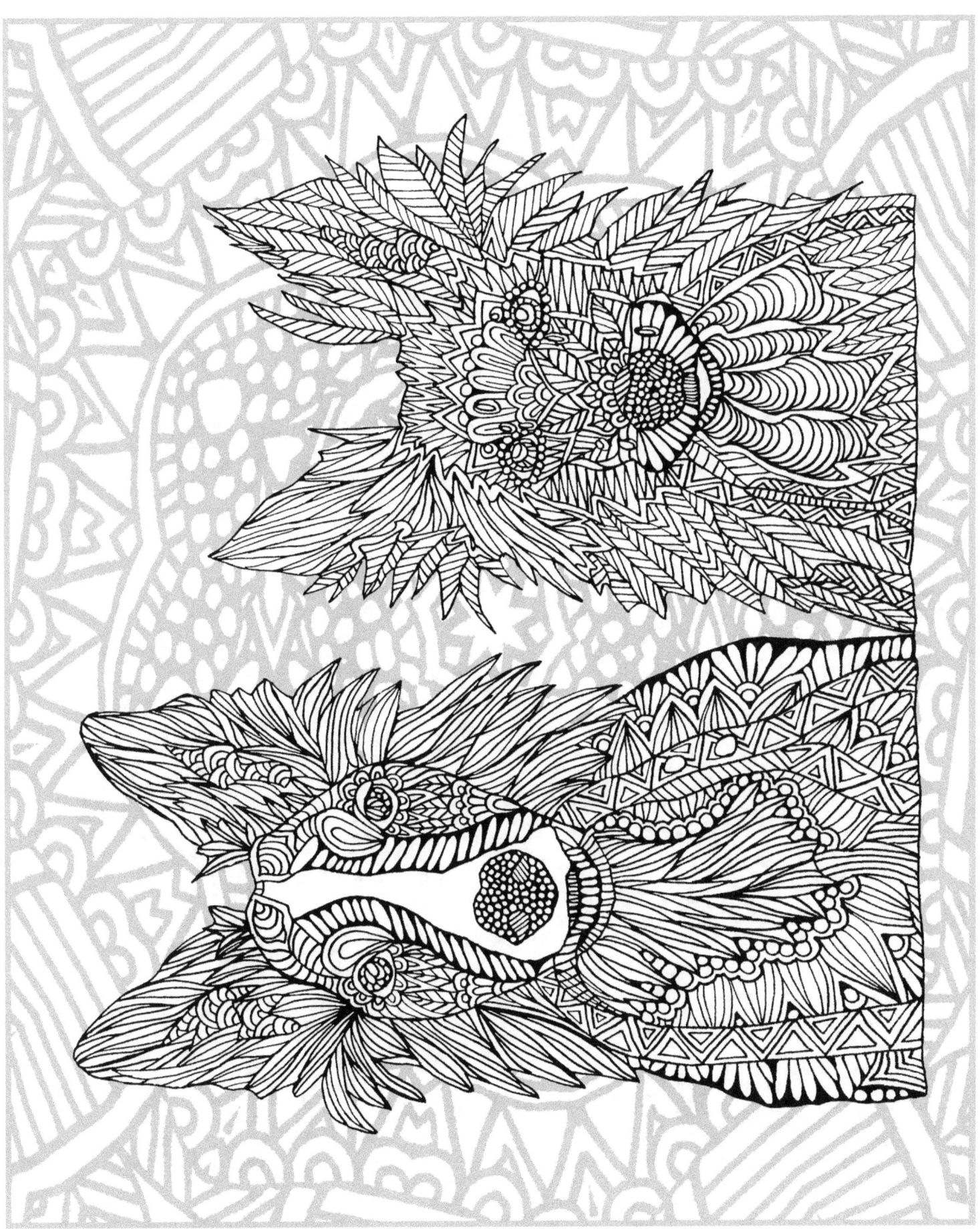

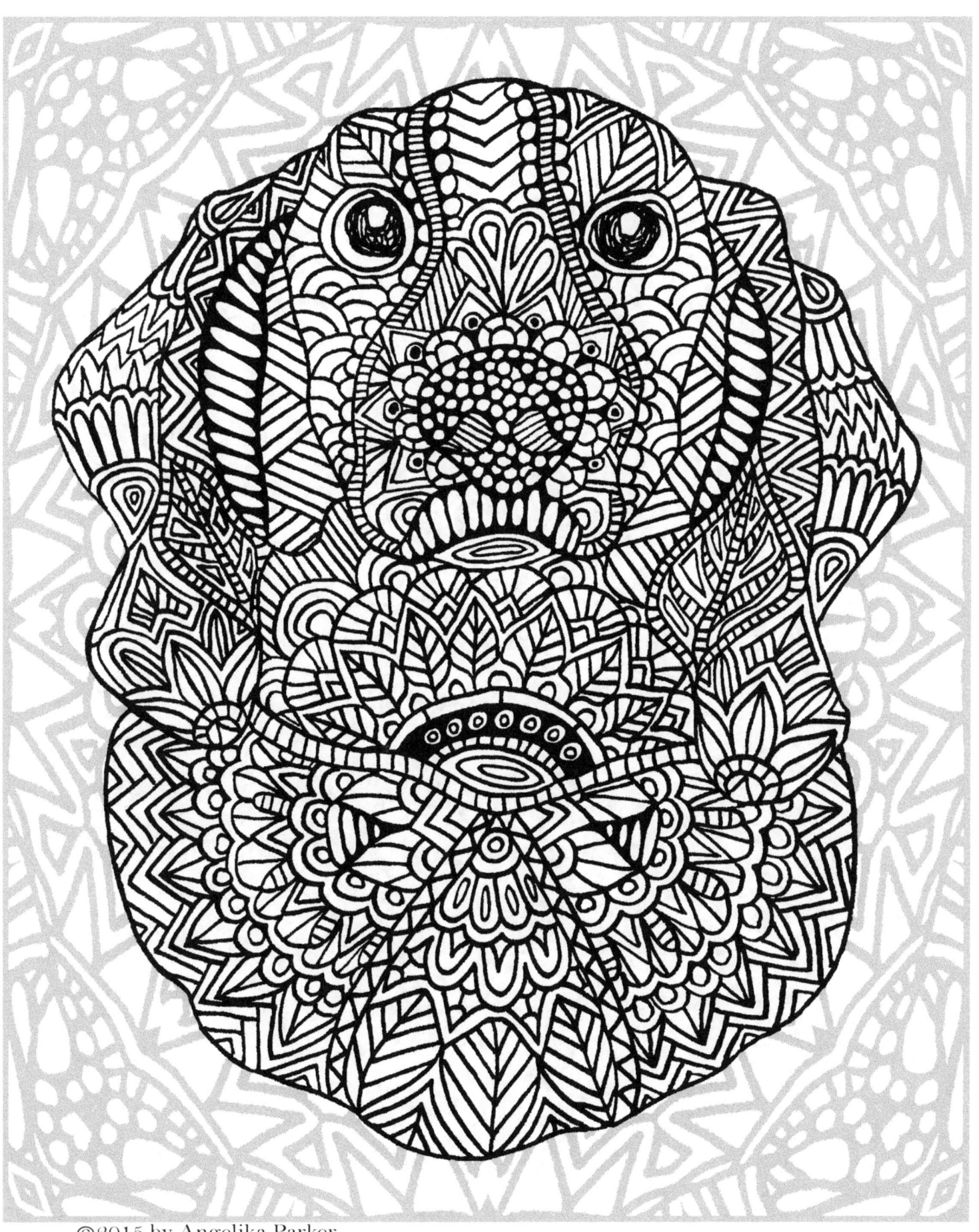

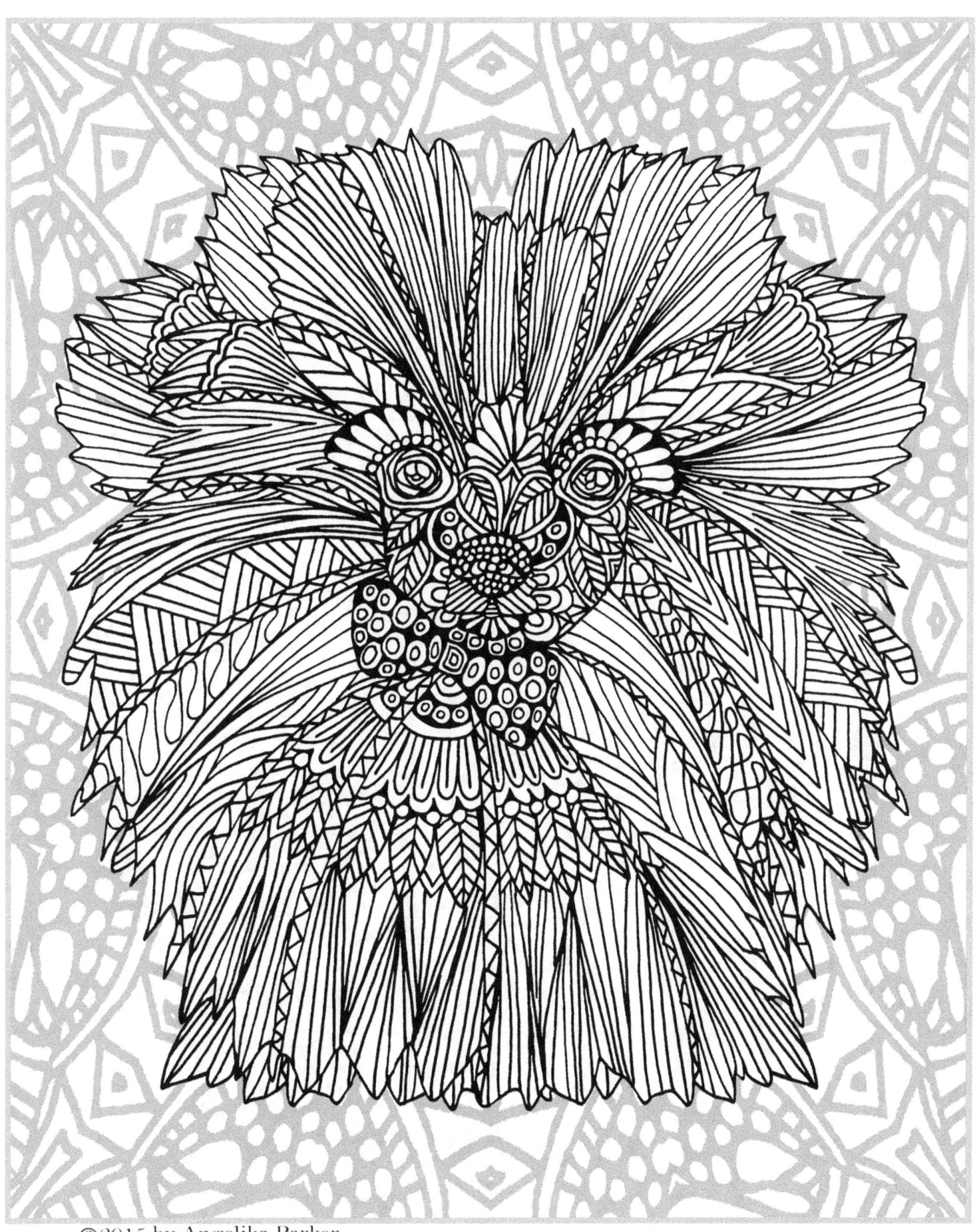

©2015 by Angelika Parker

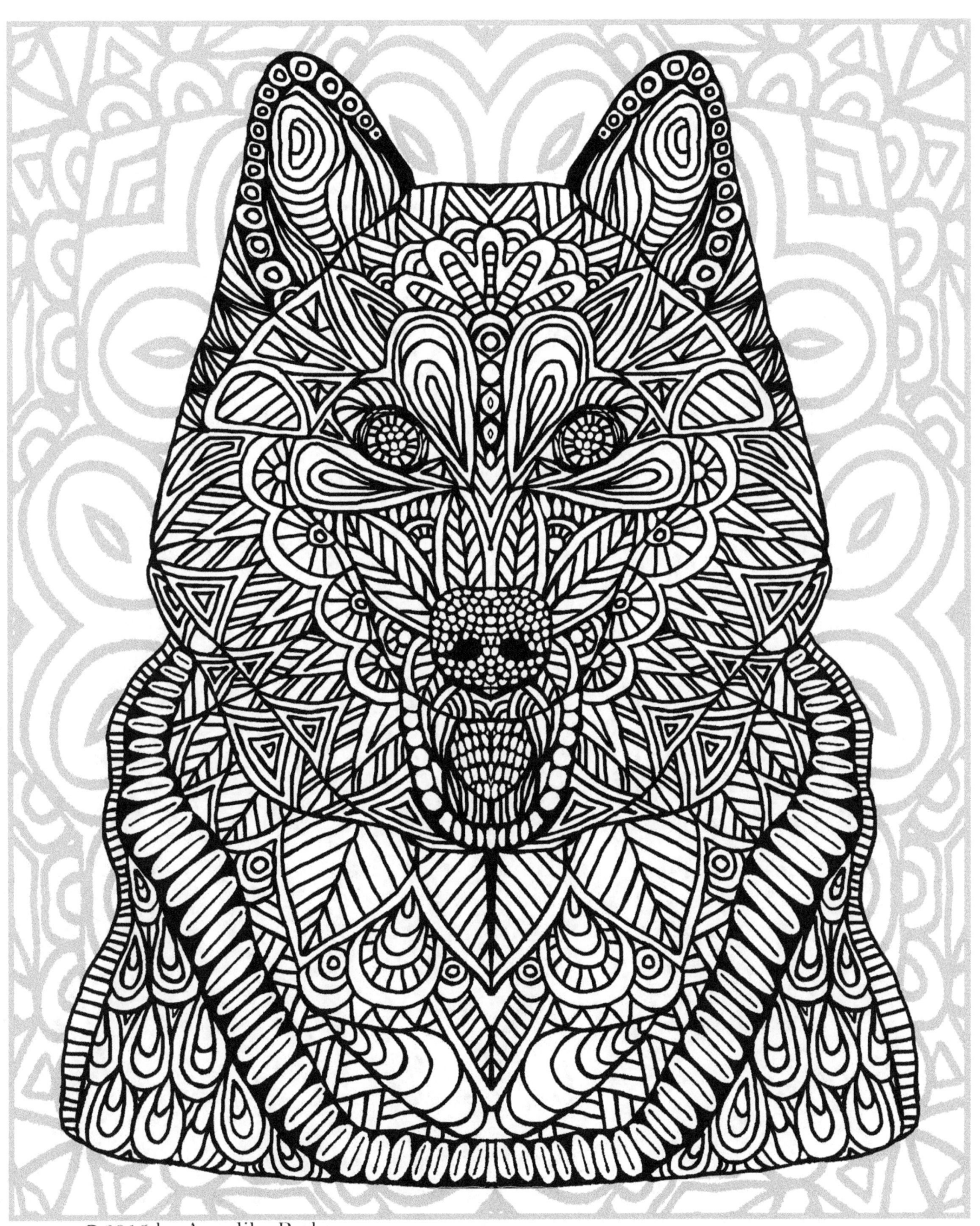

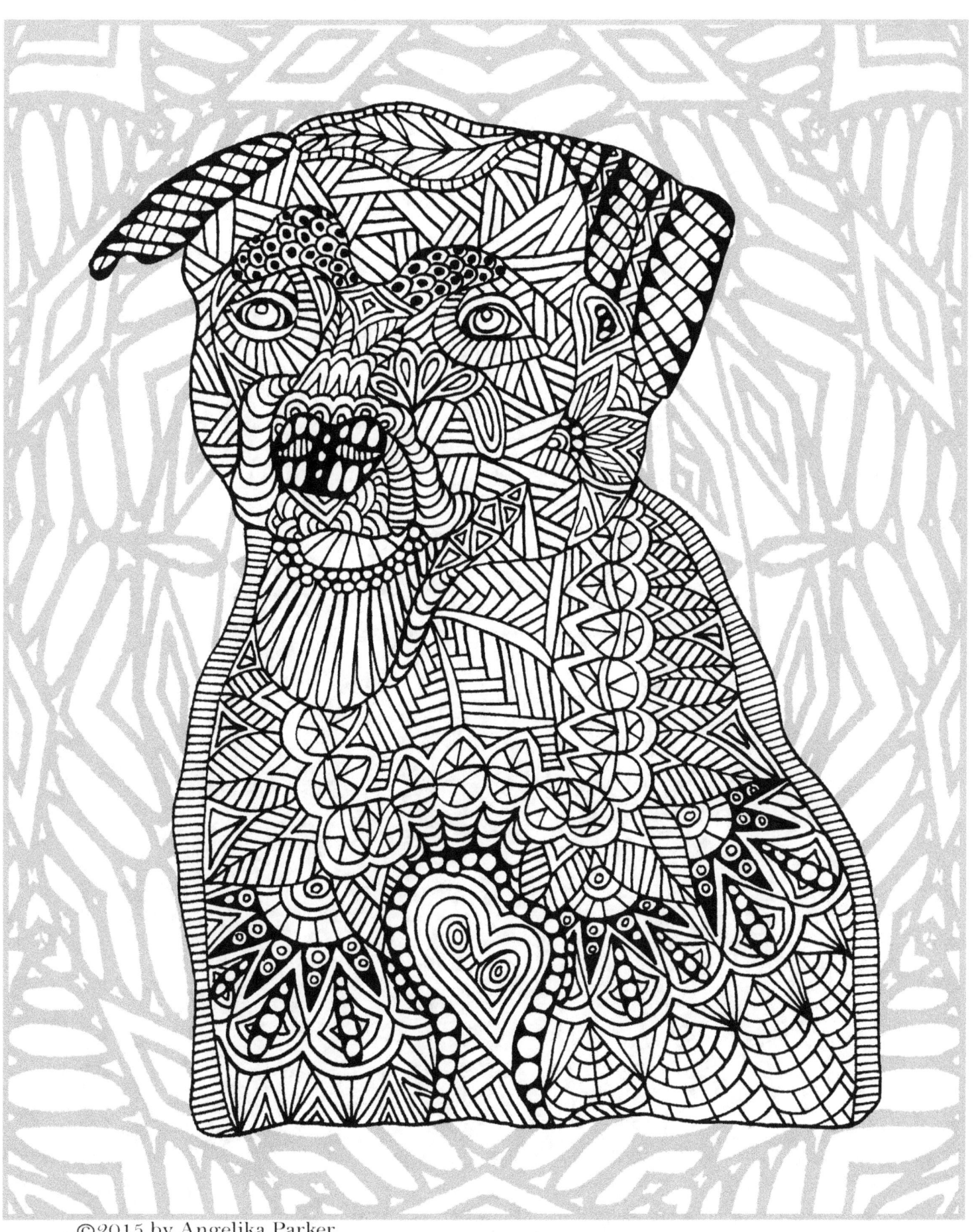

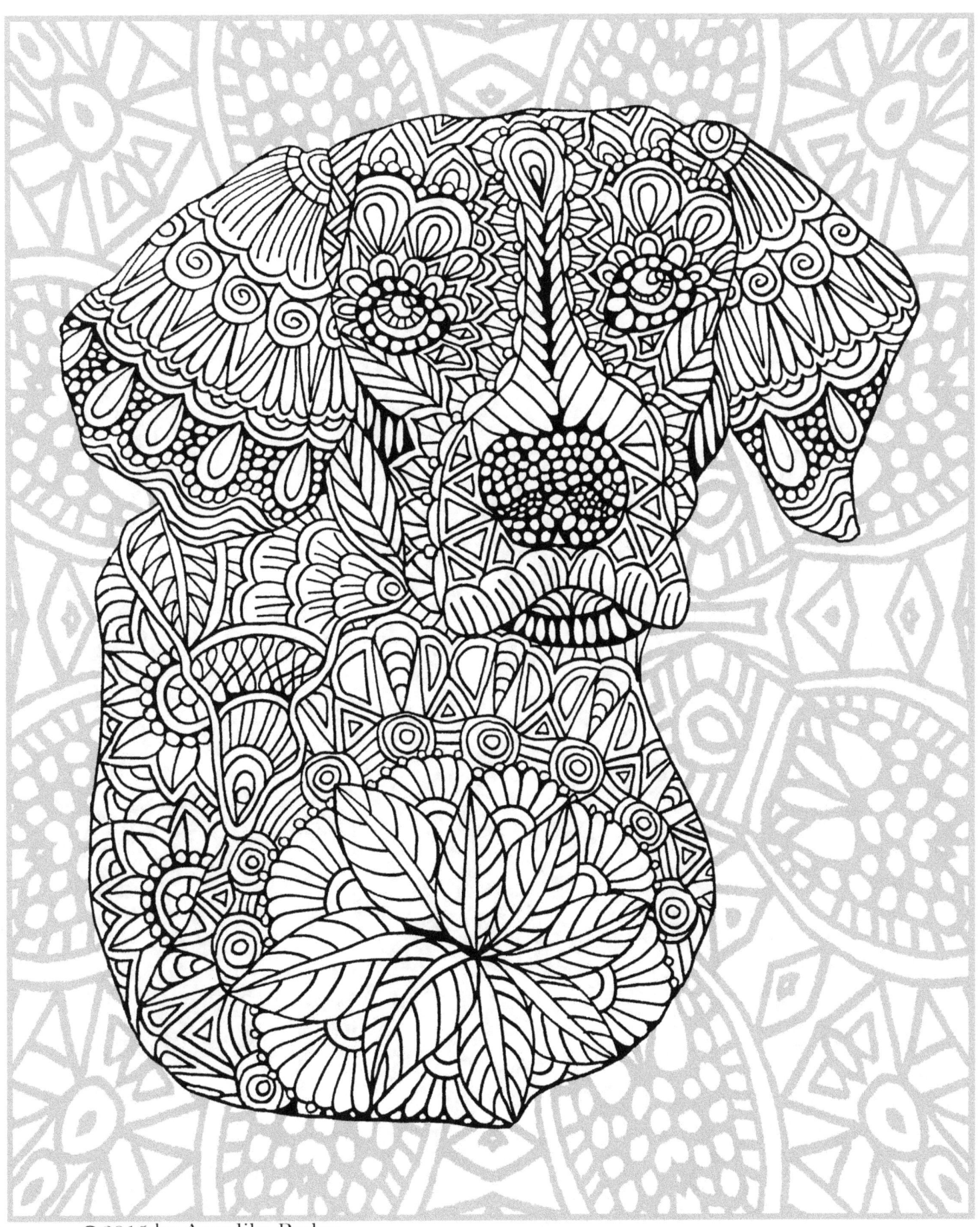

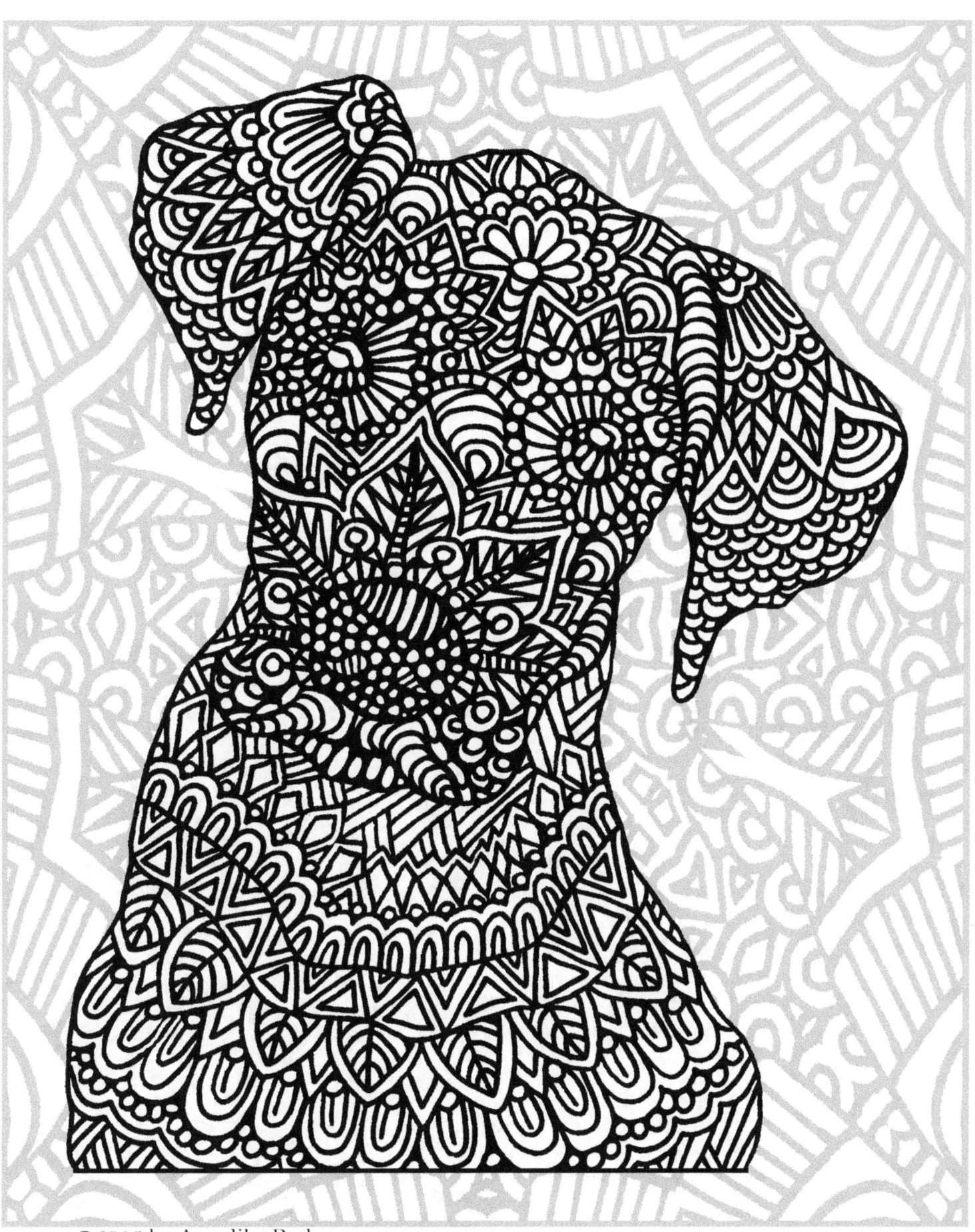

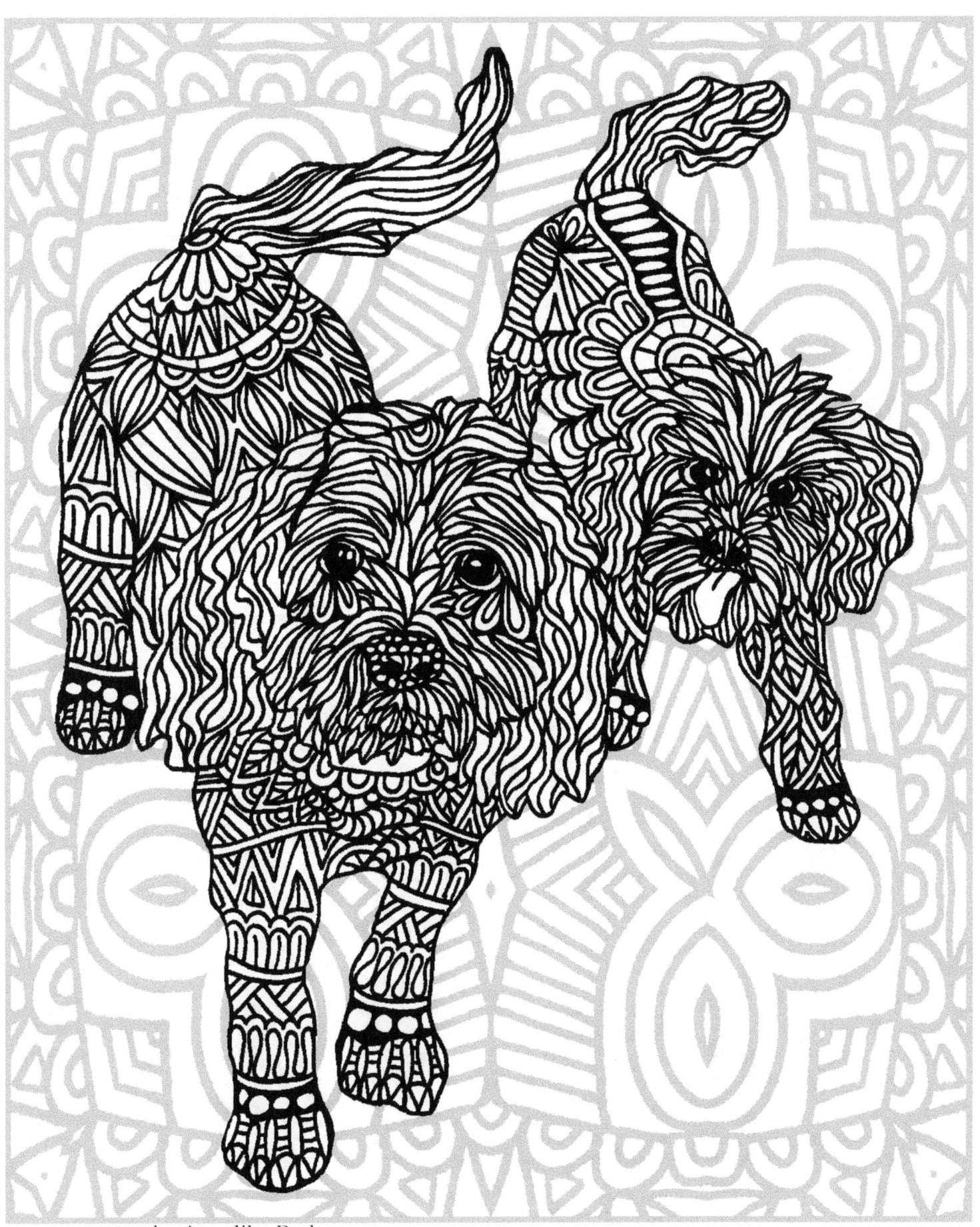

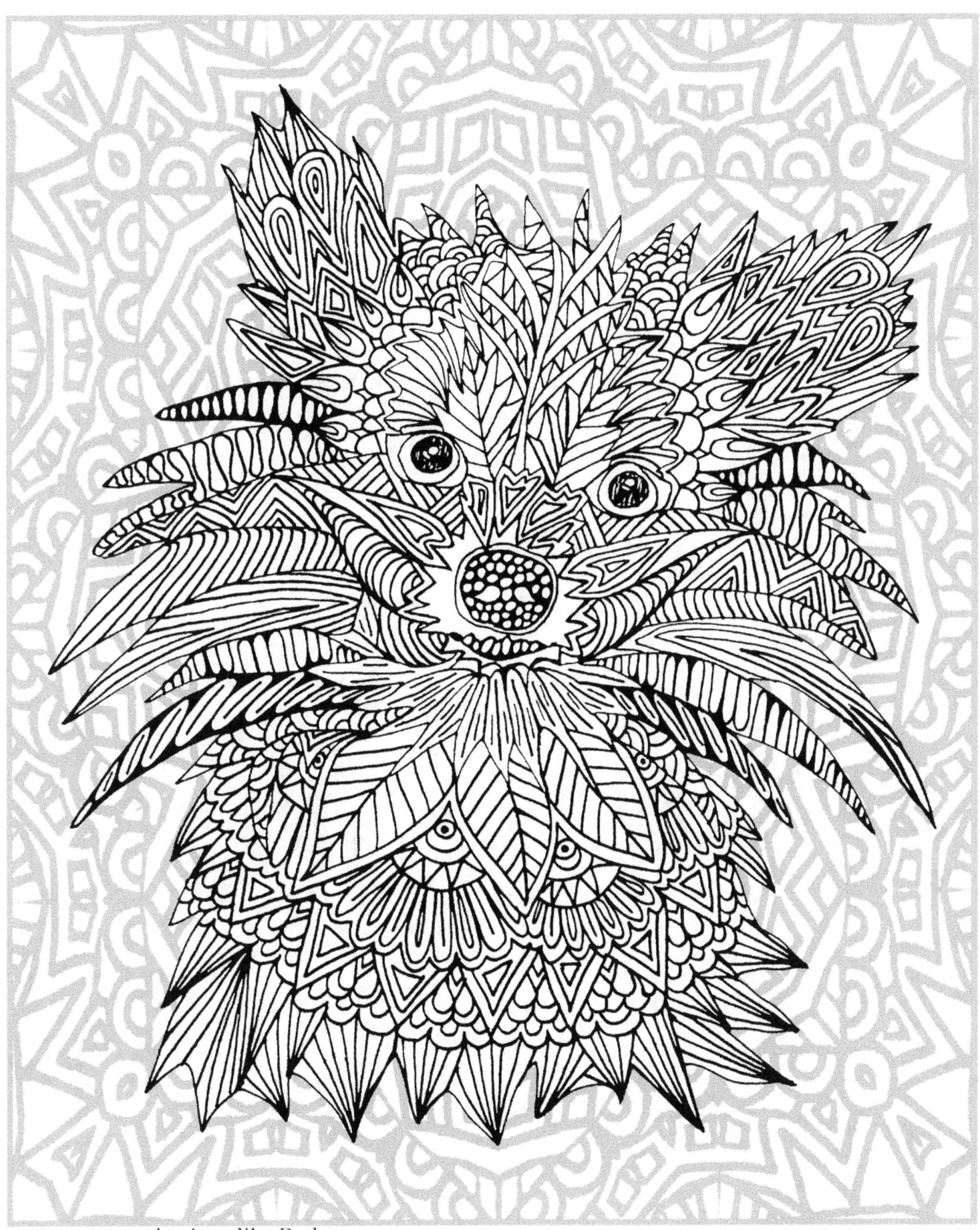

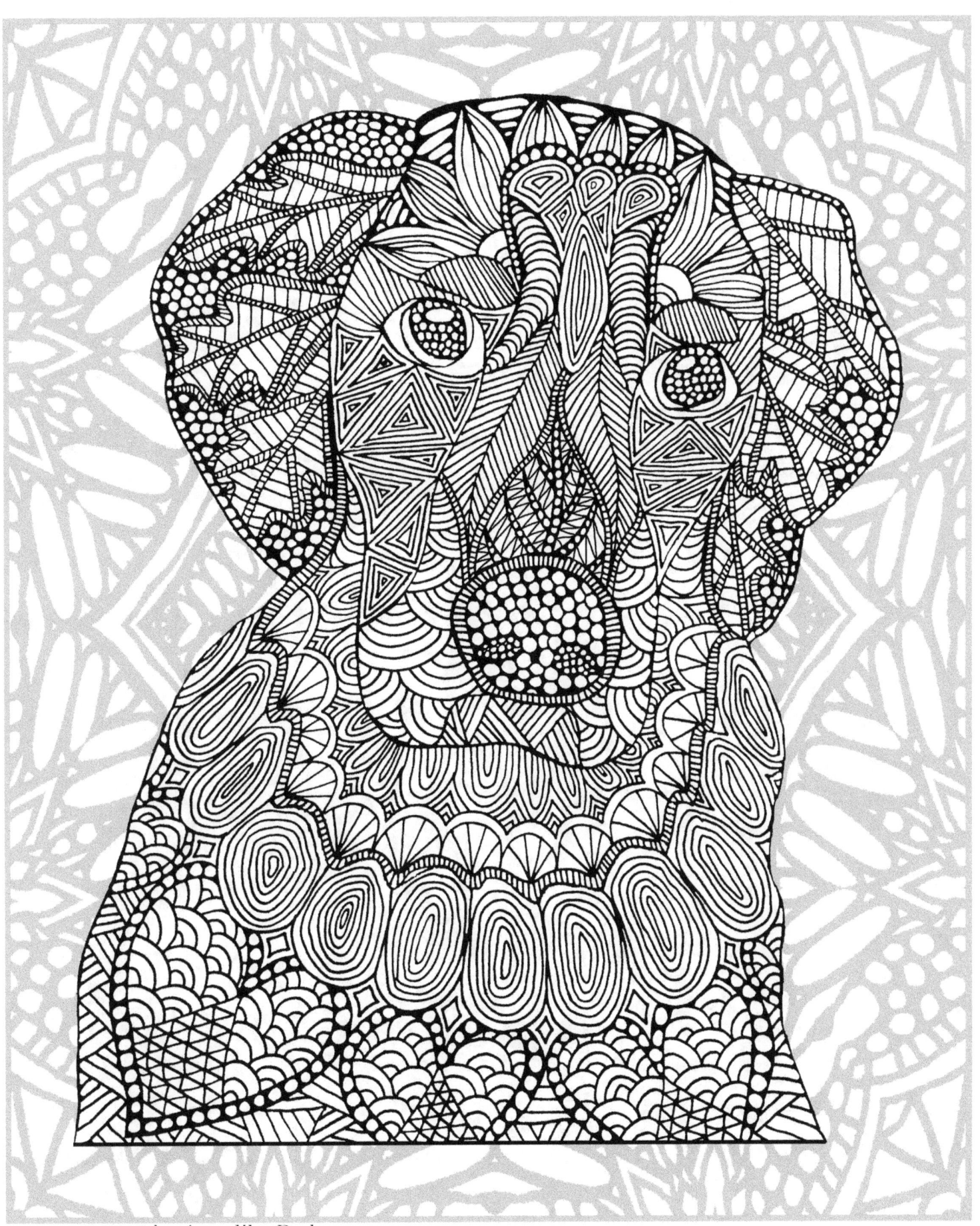

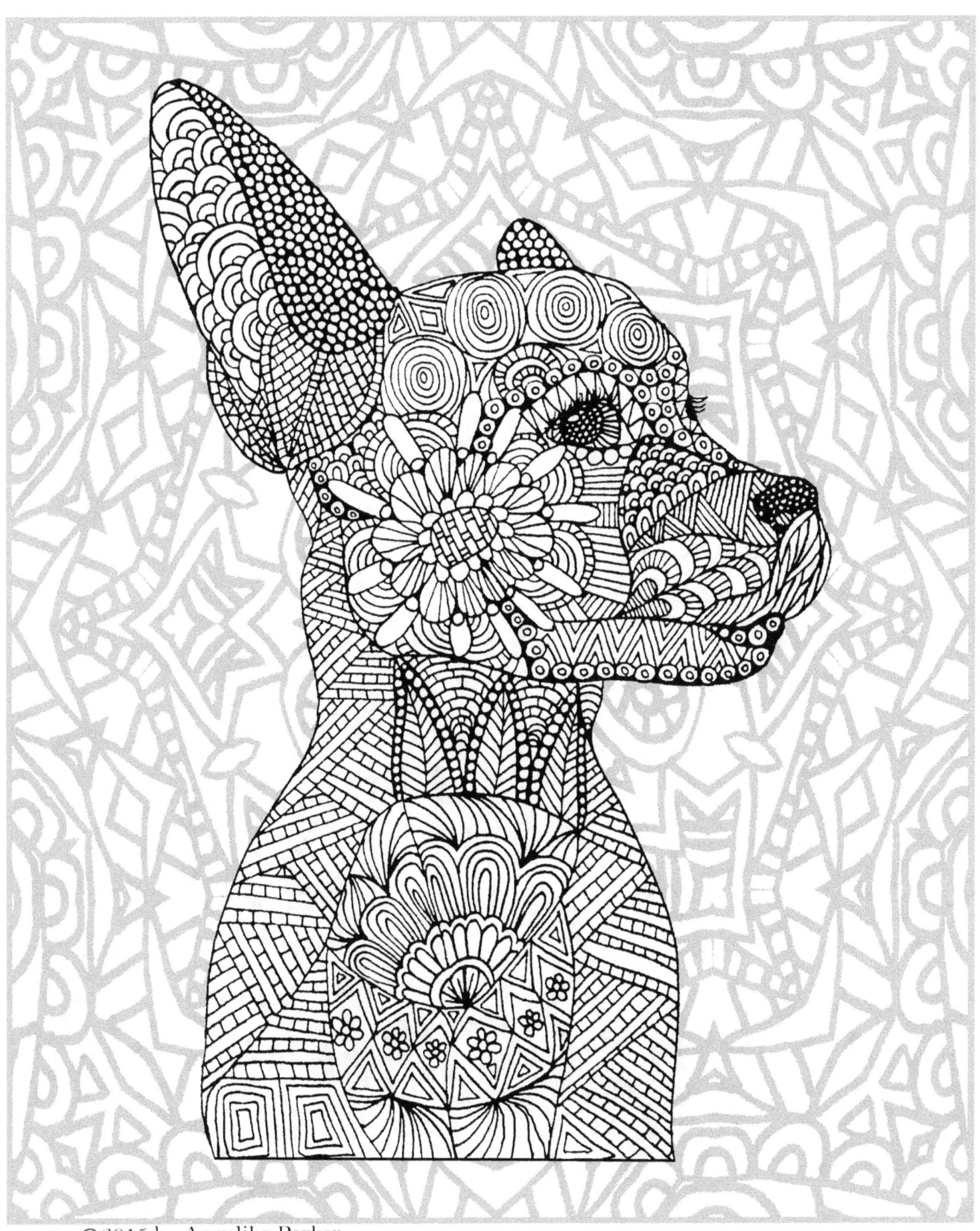

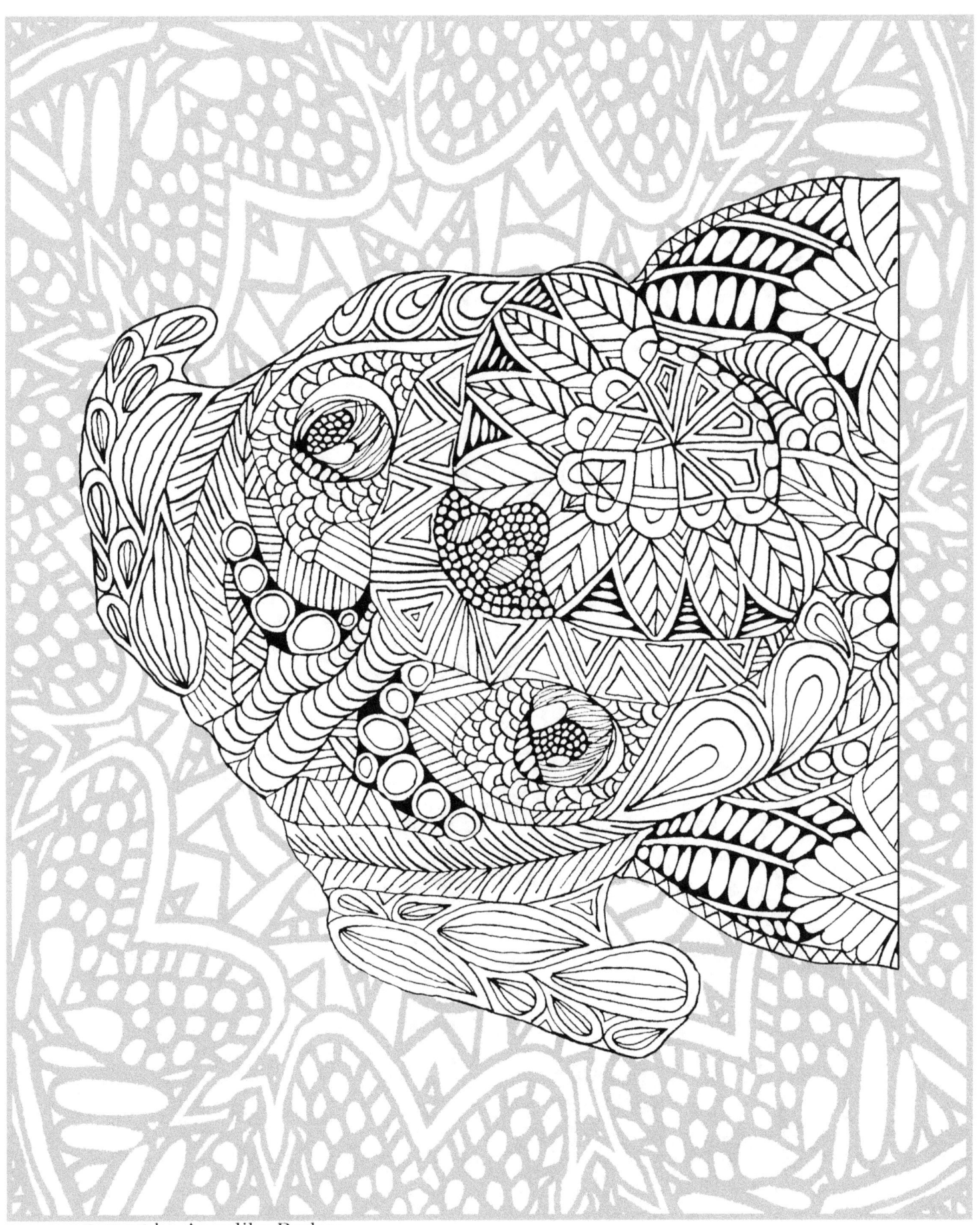

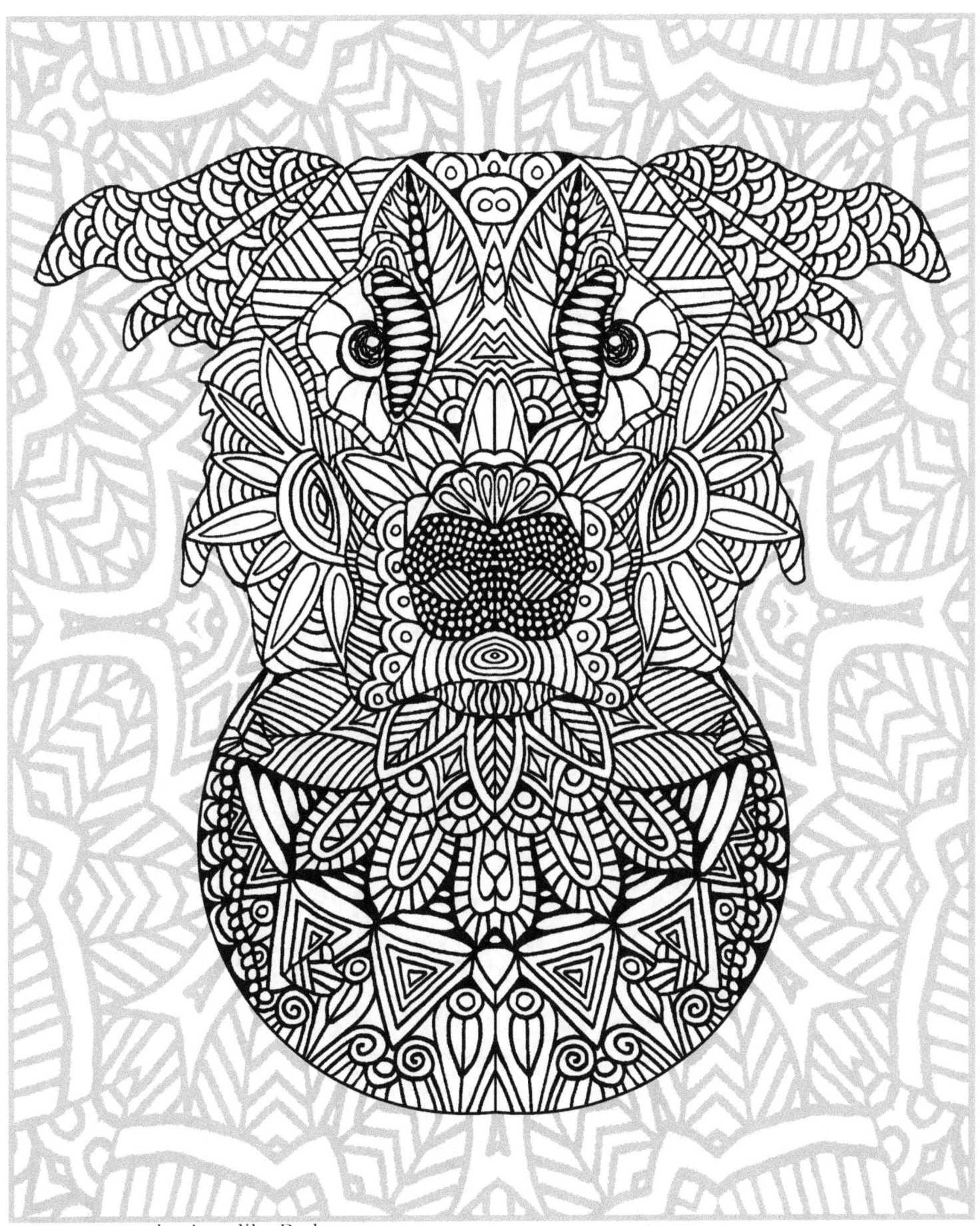

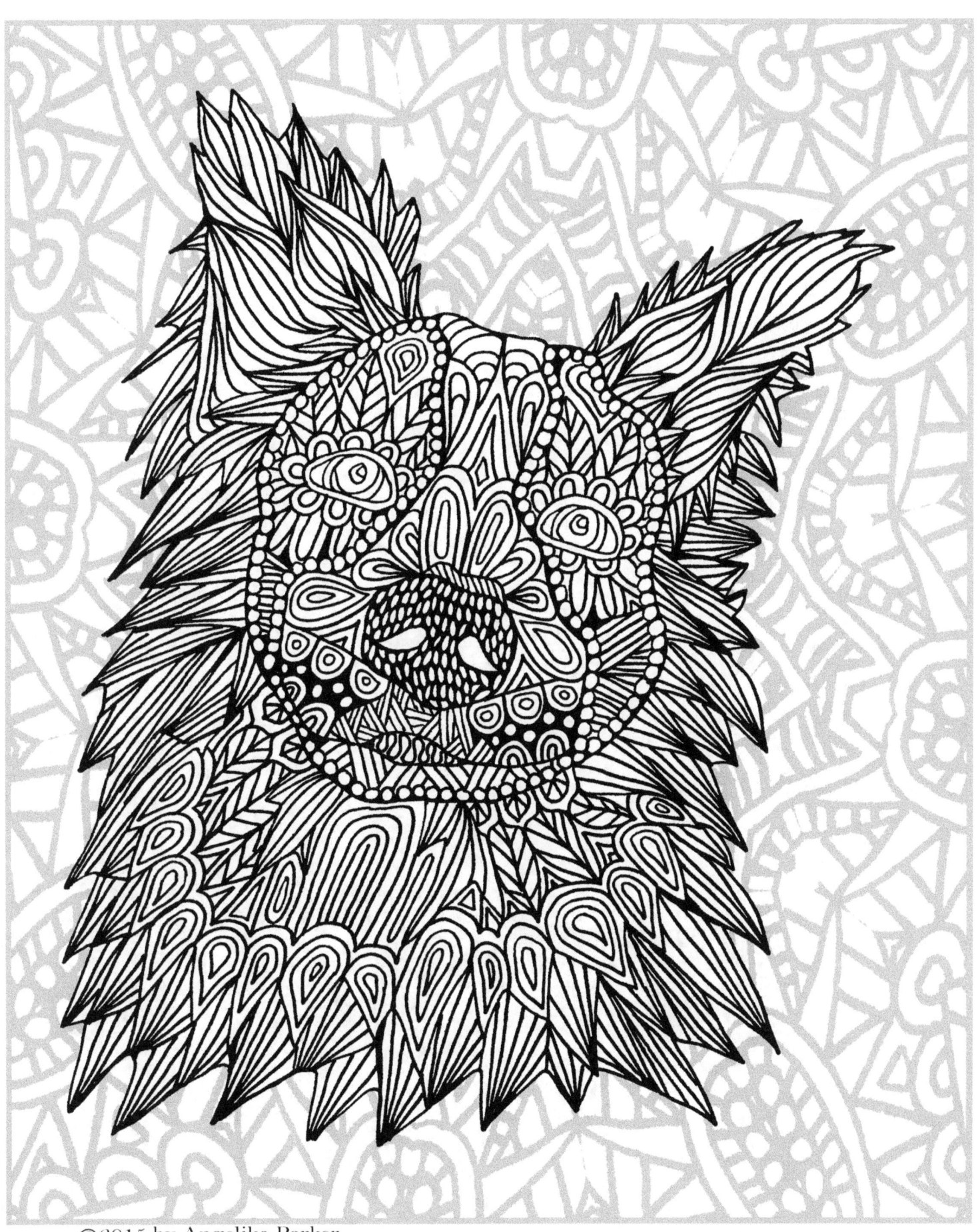

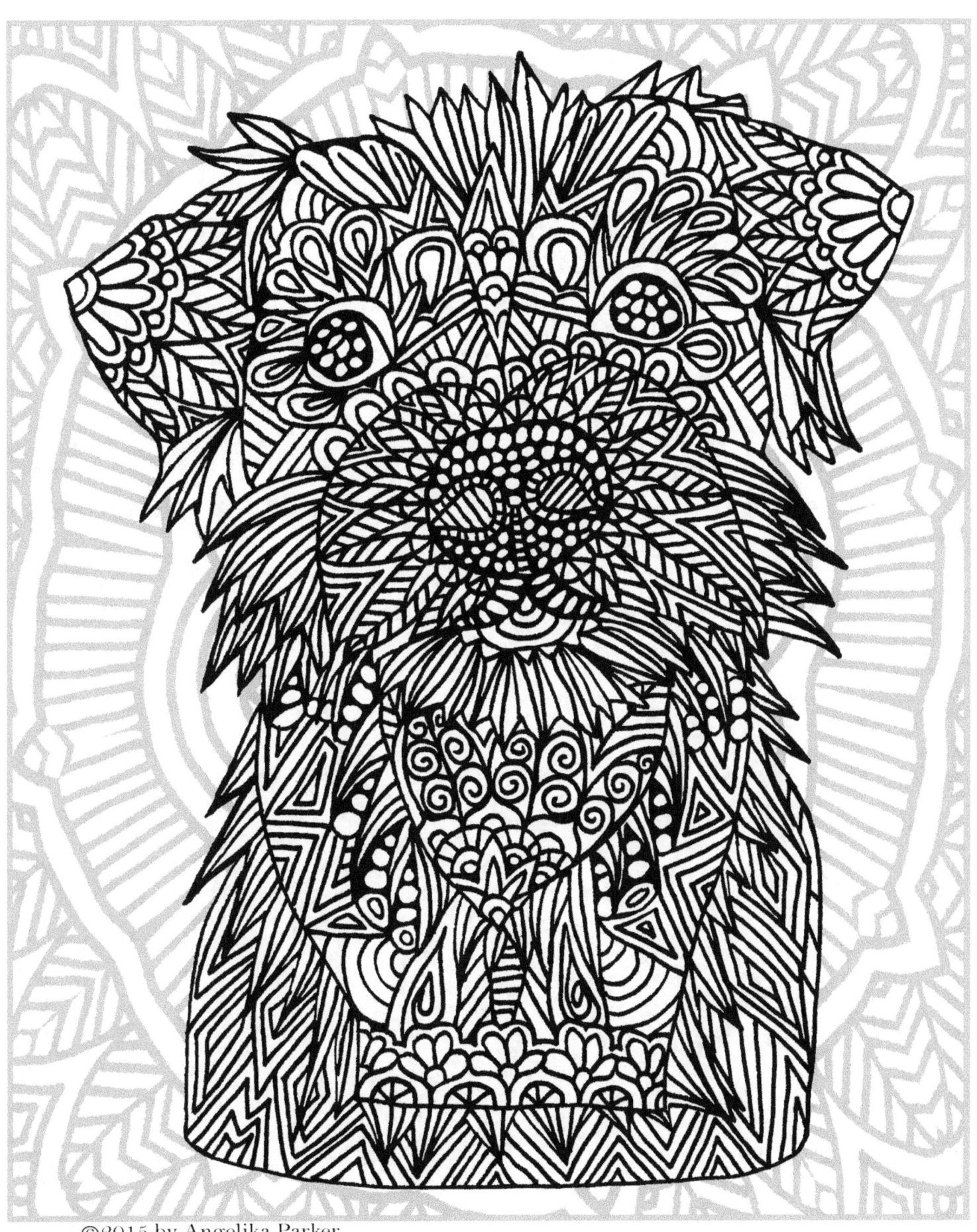

©2015 by Angelika Parker

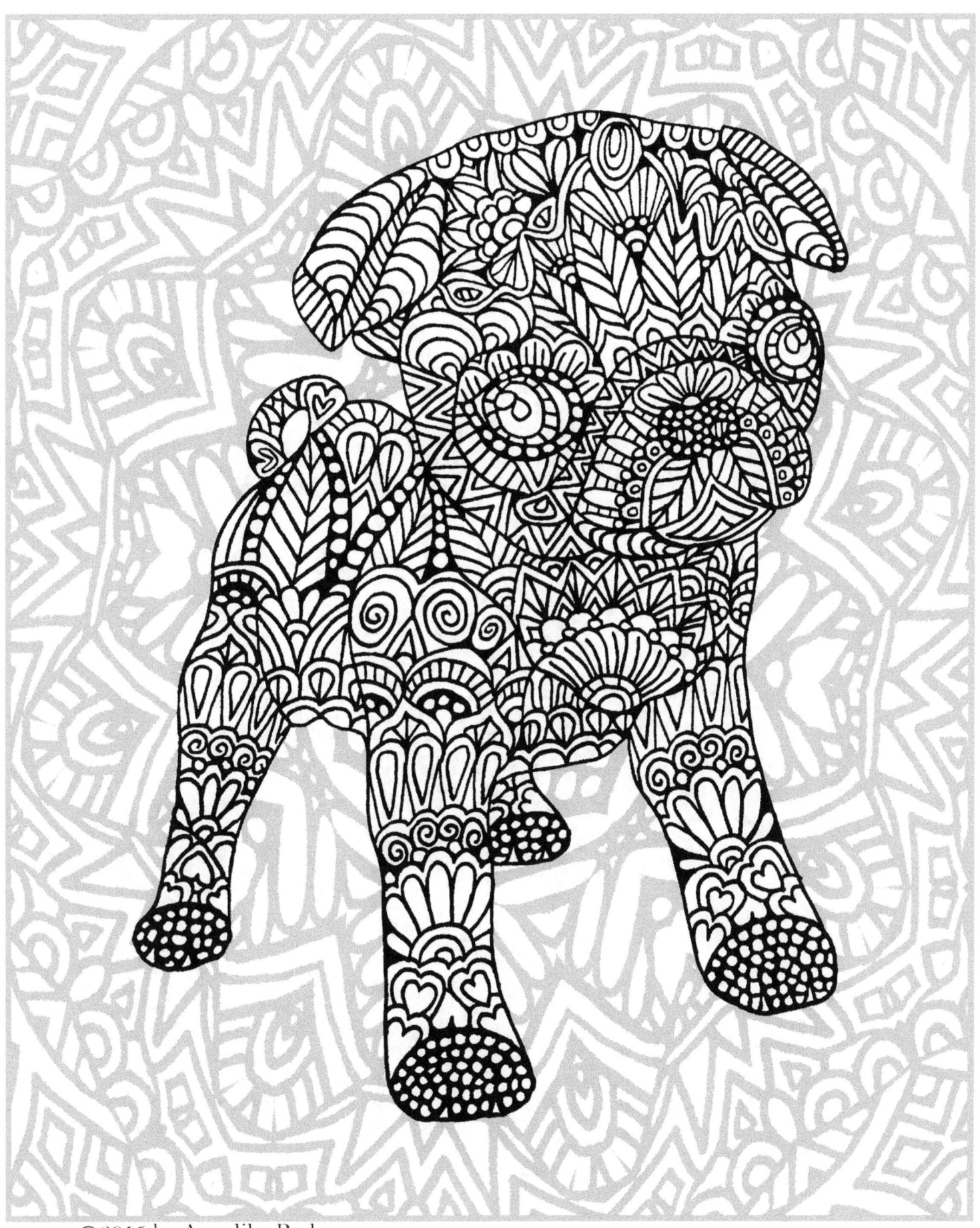

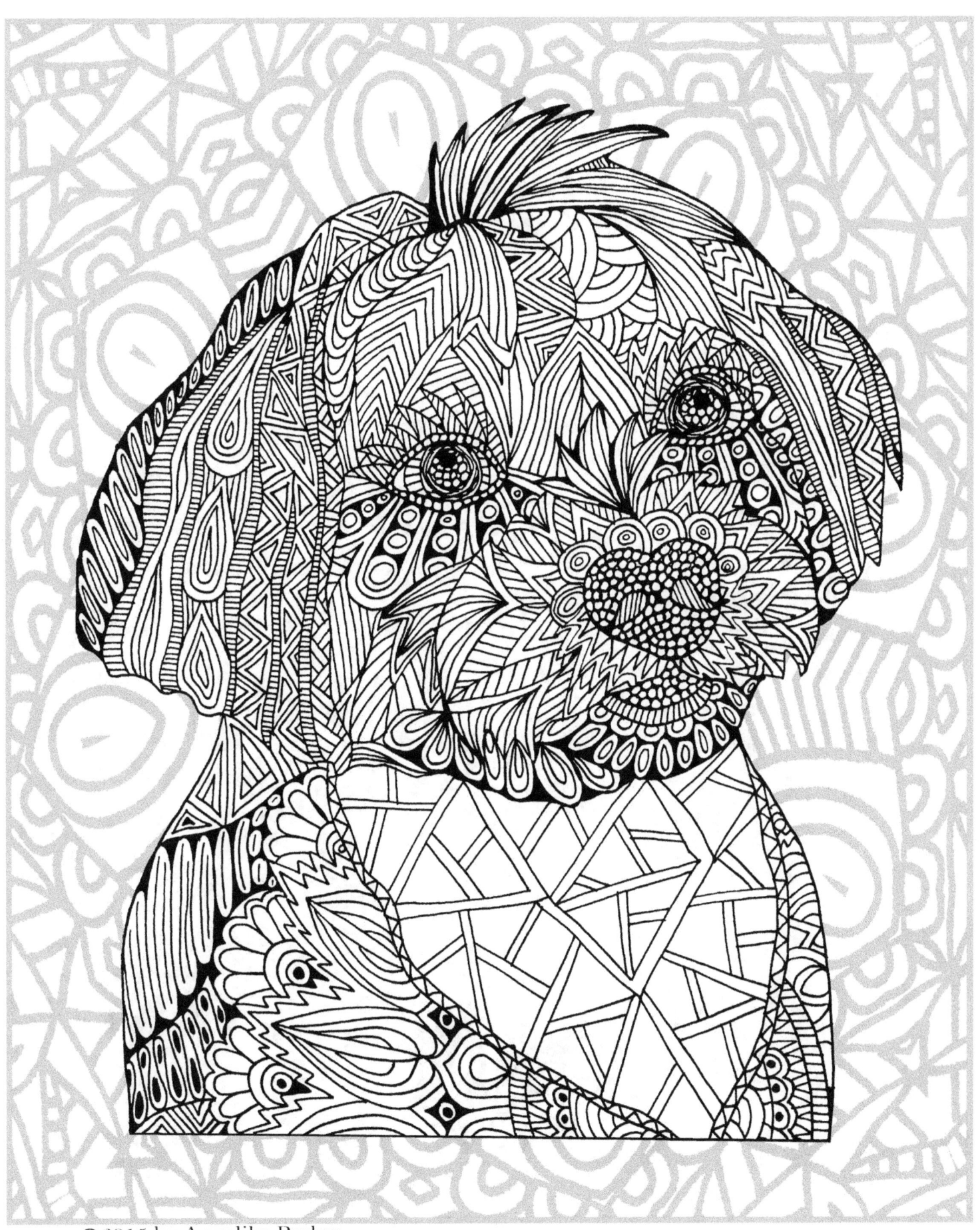

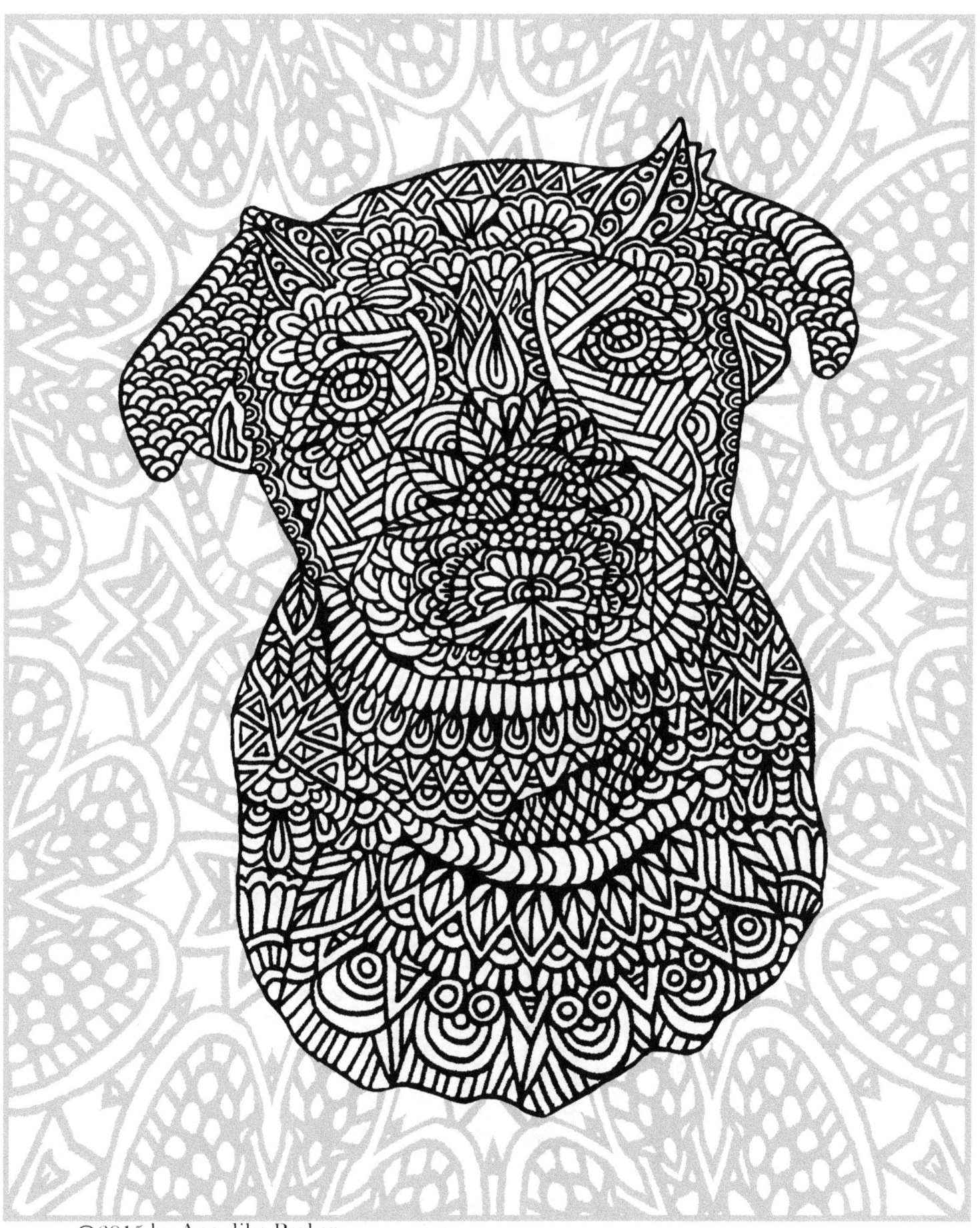

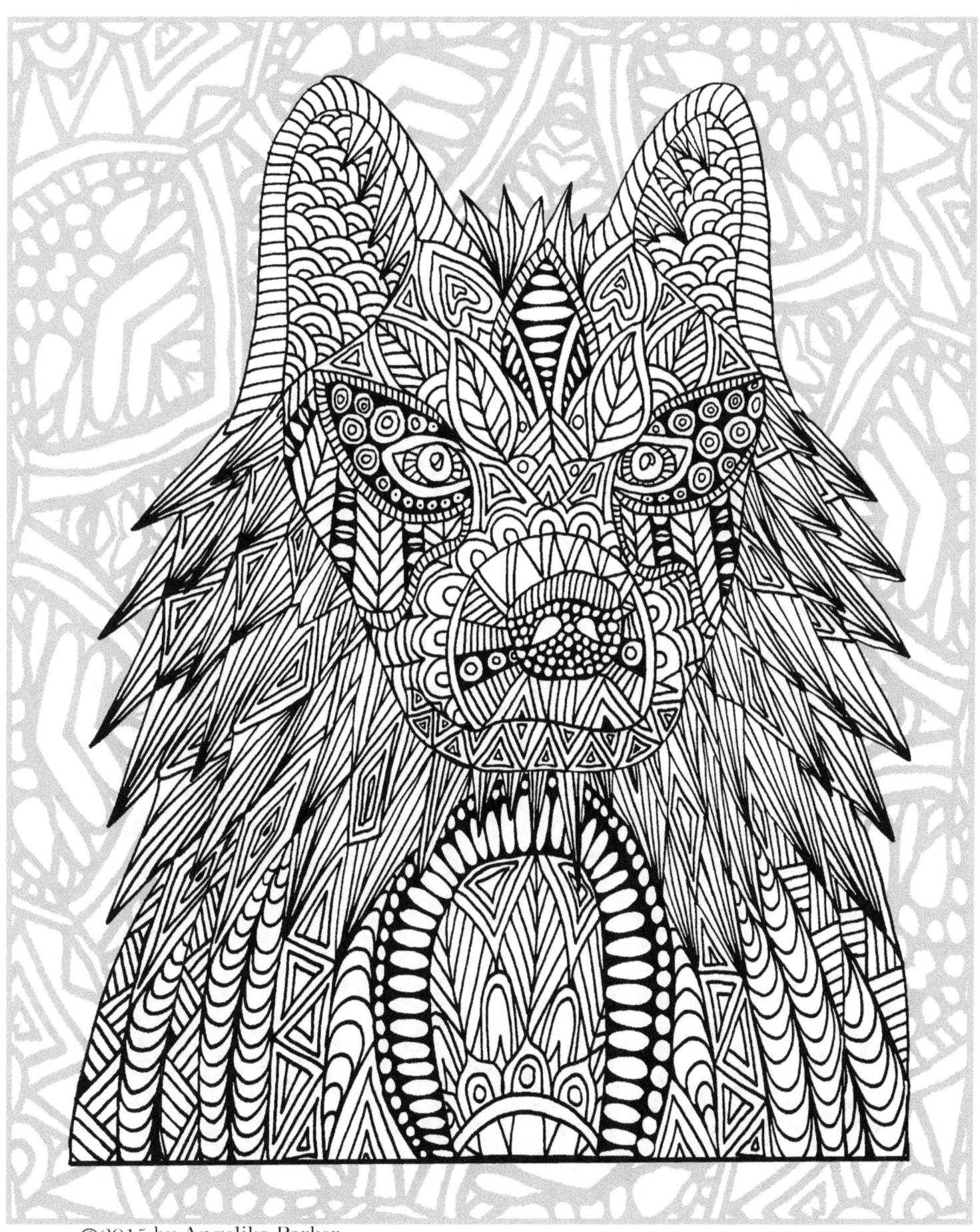

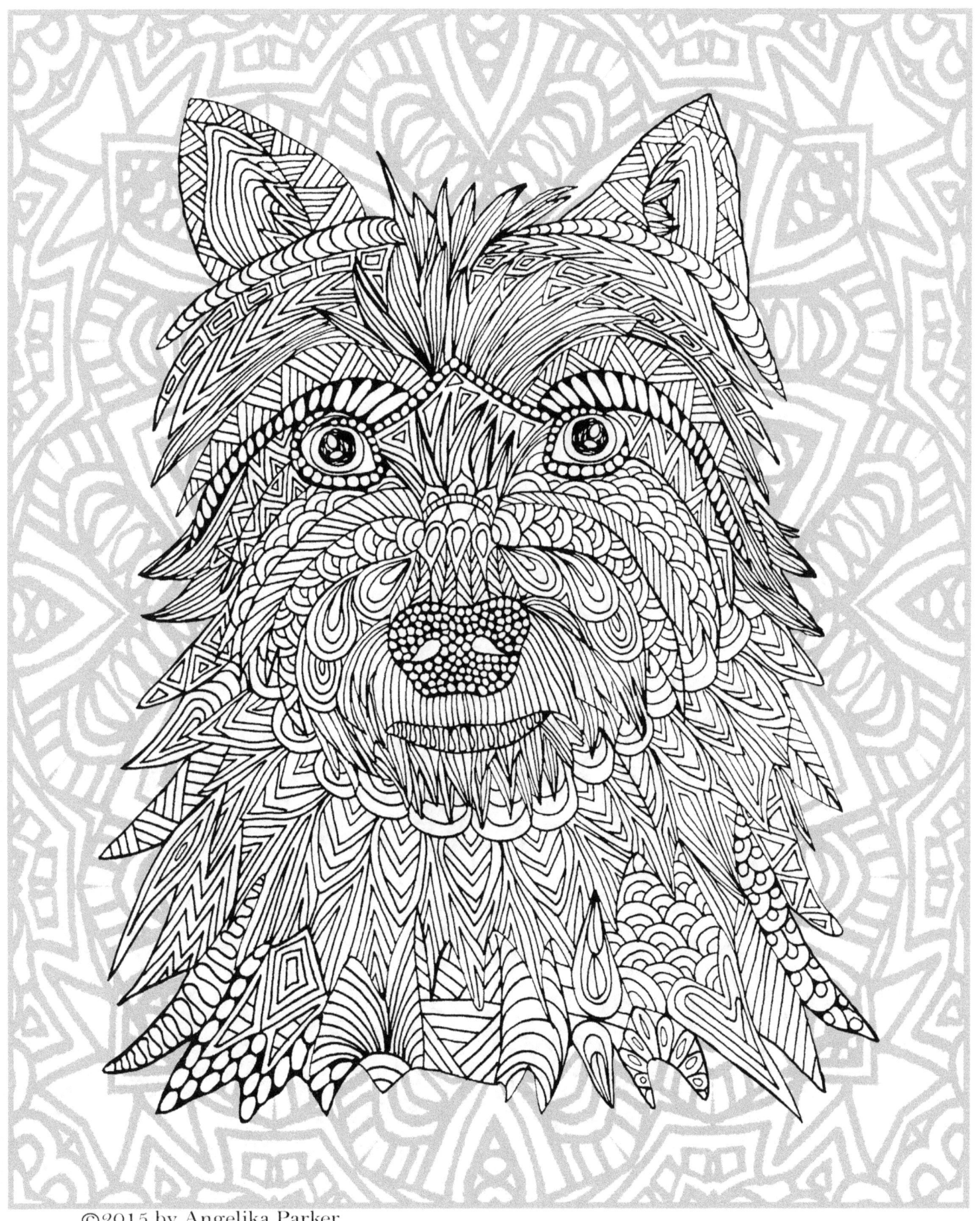

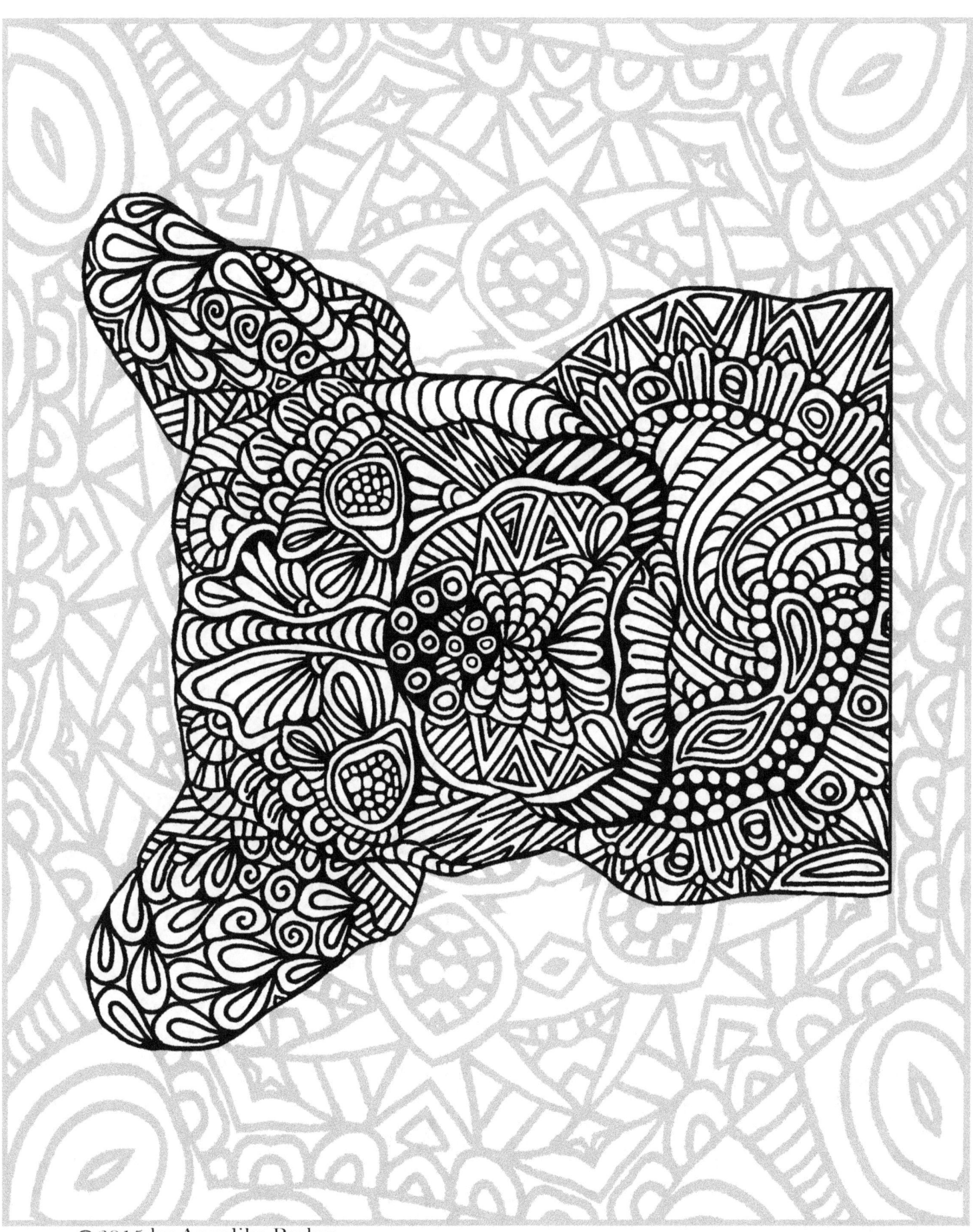

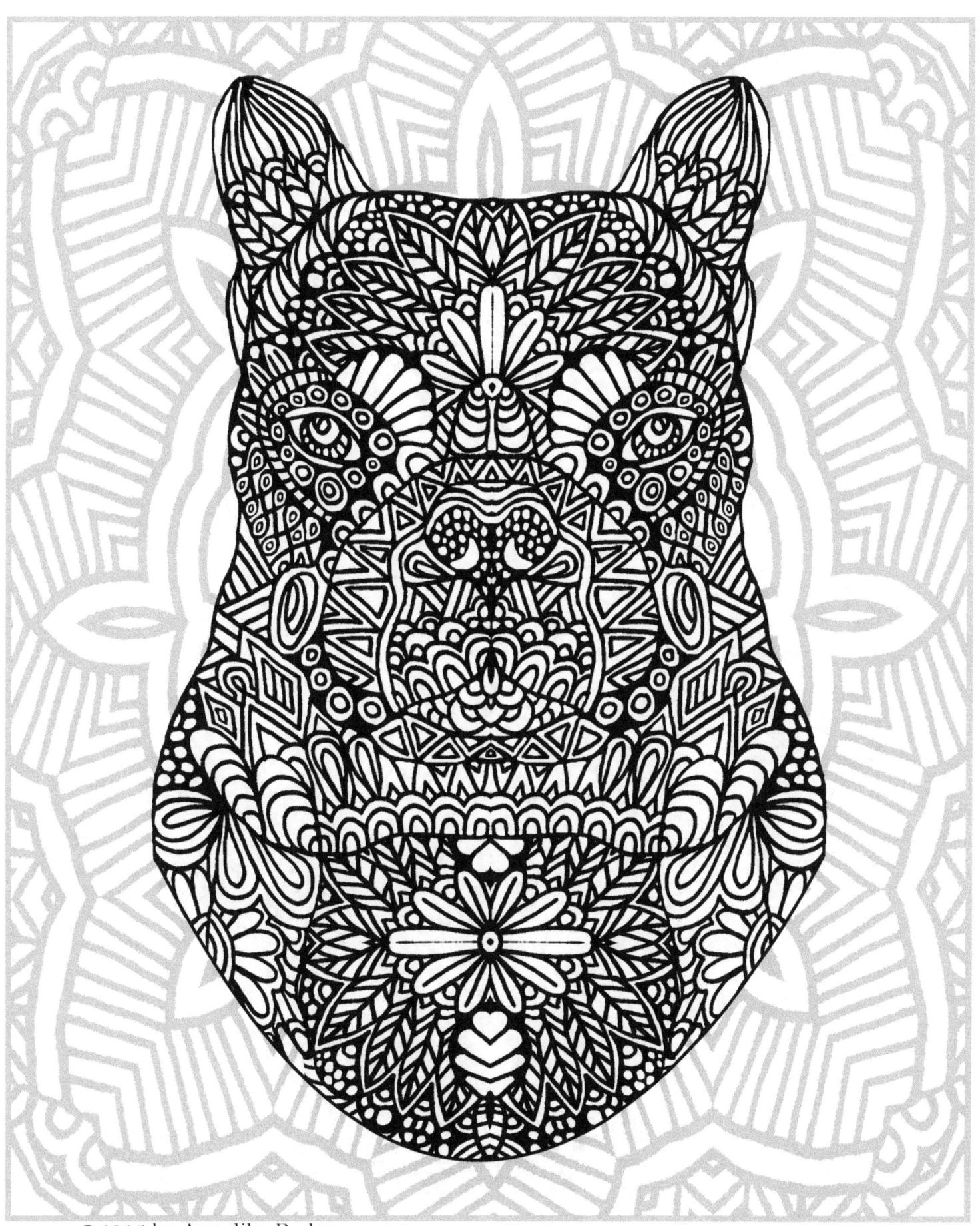

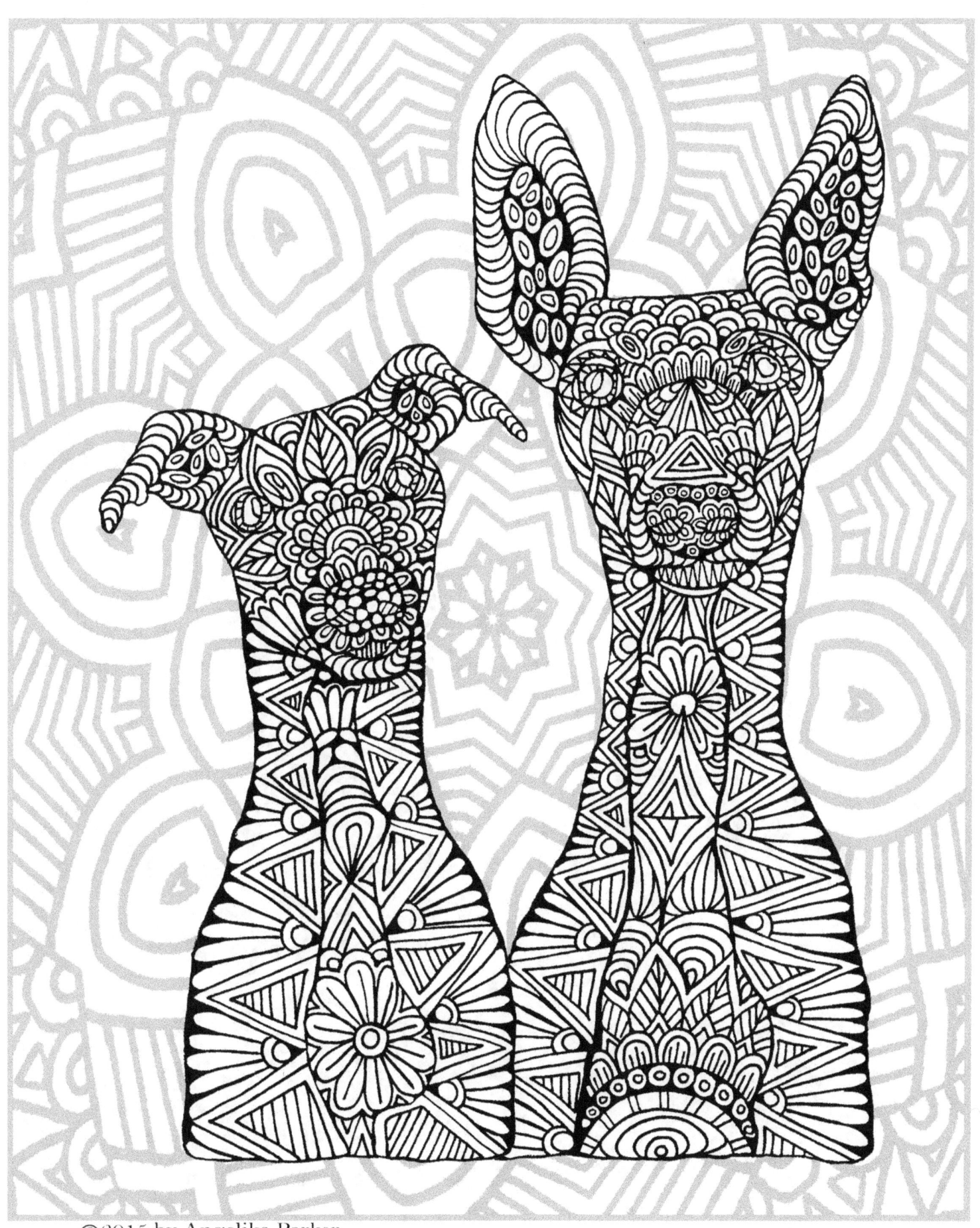

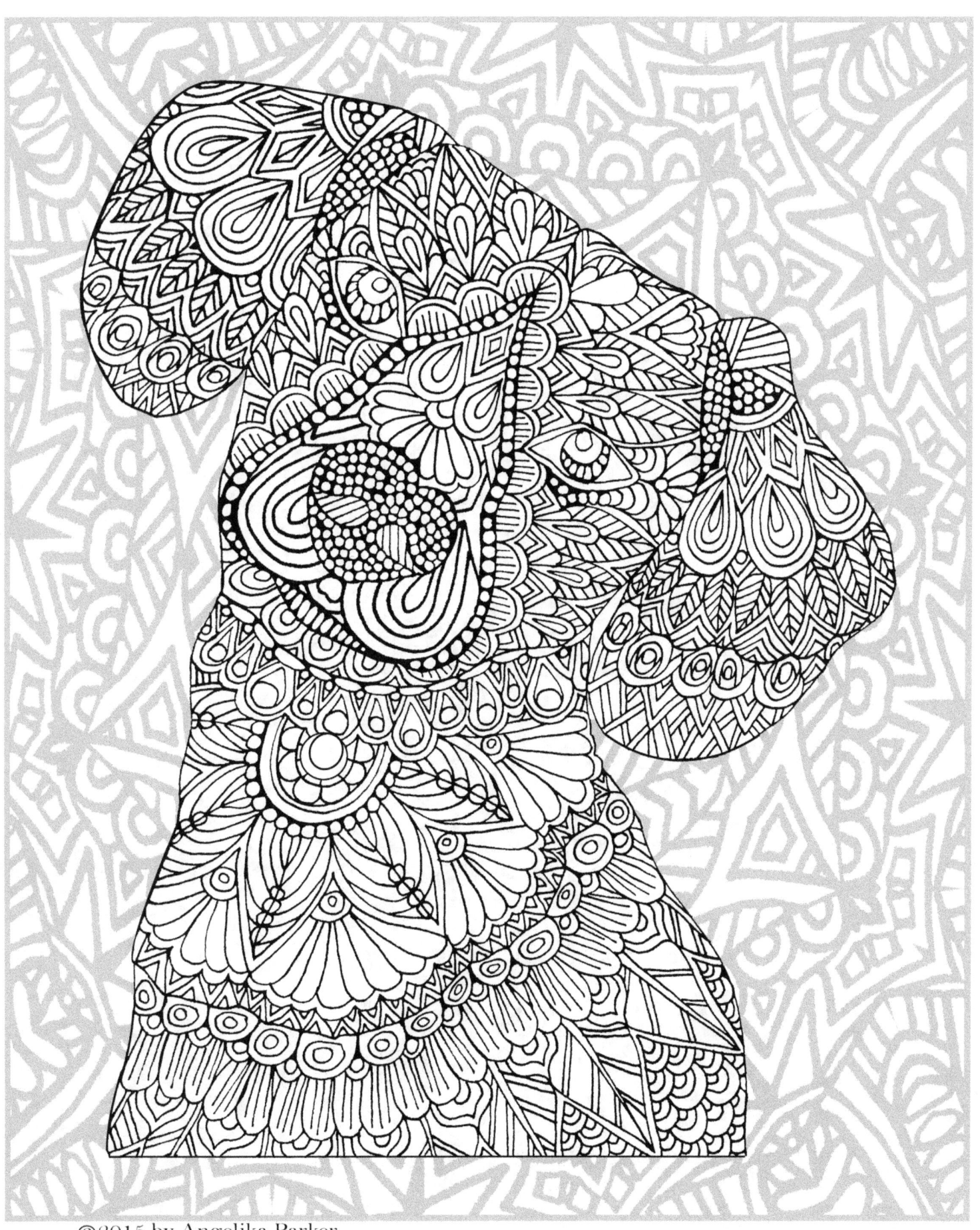

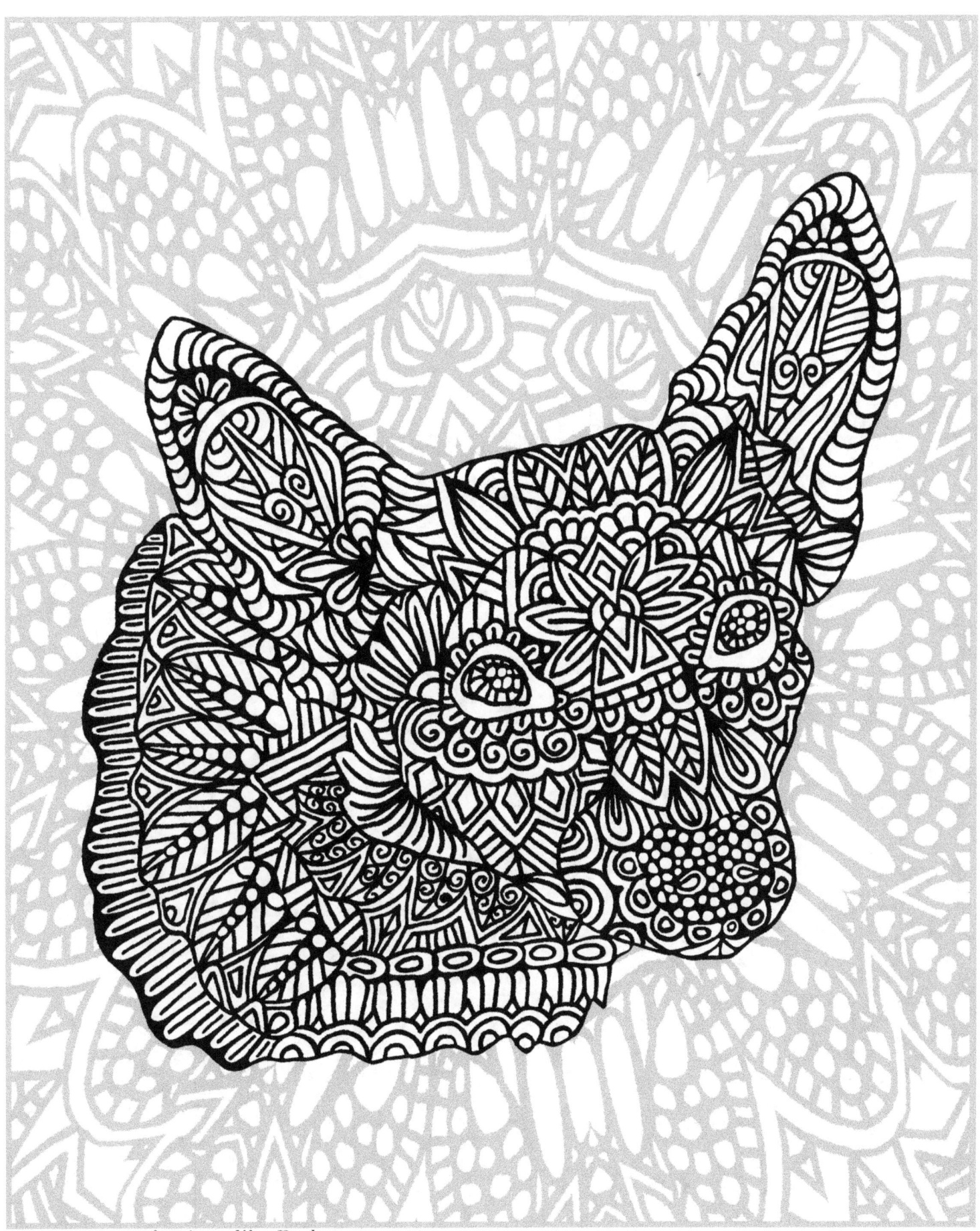

©2015 by Angelika Parker

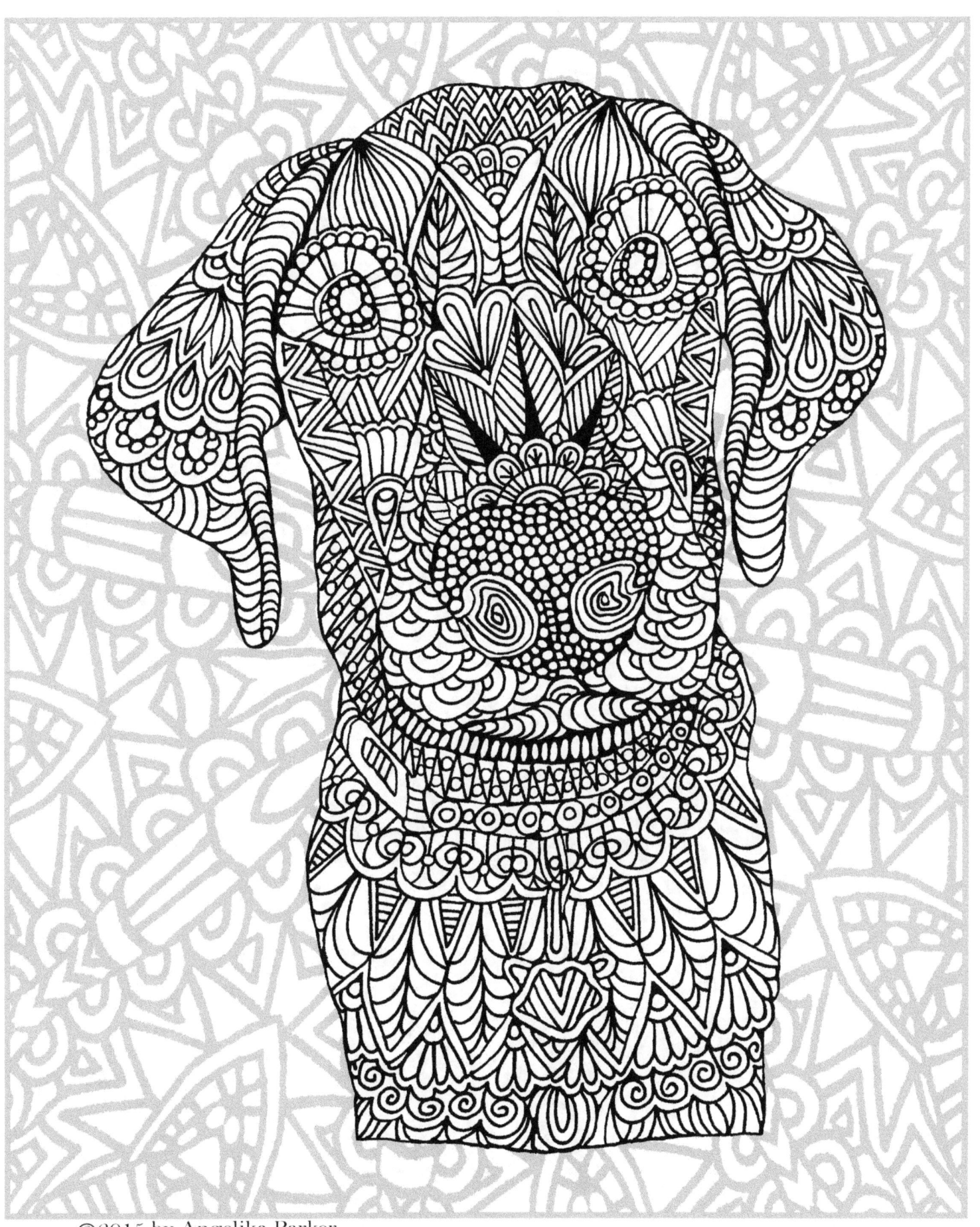

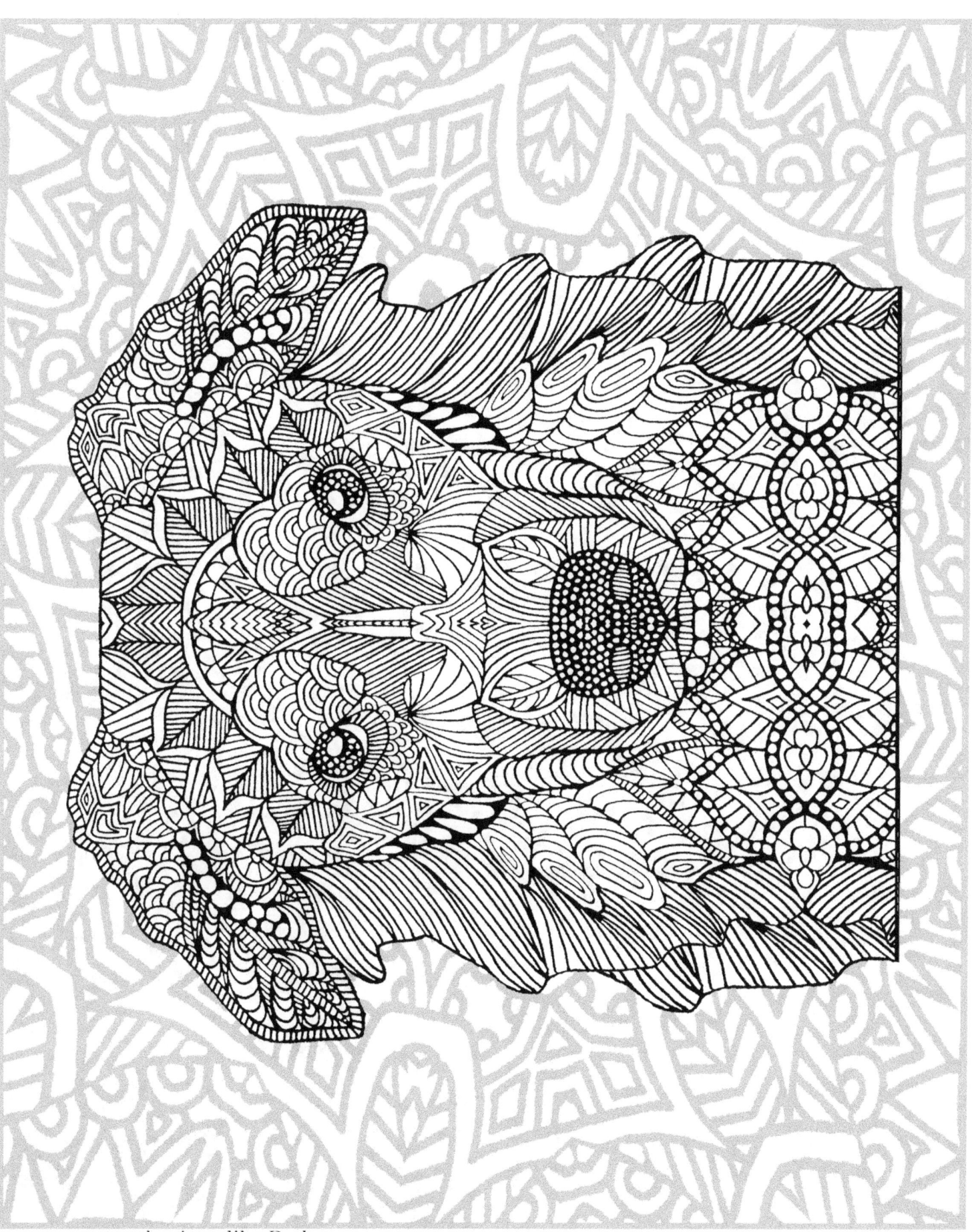

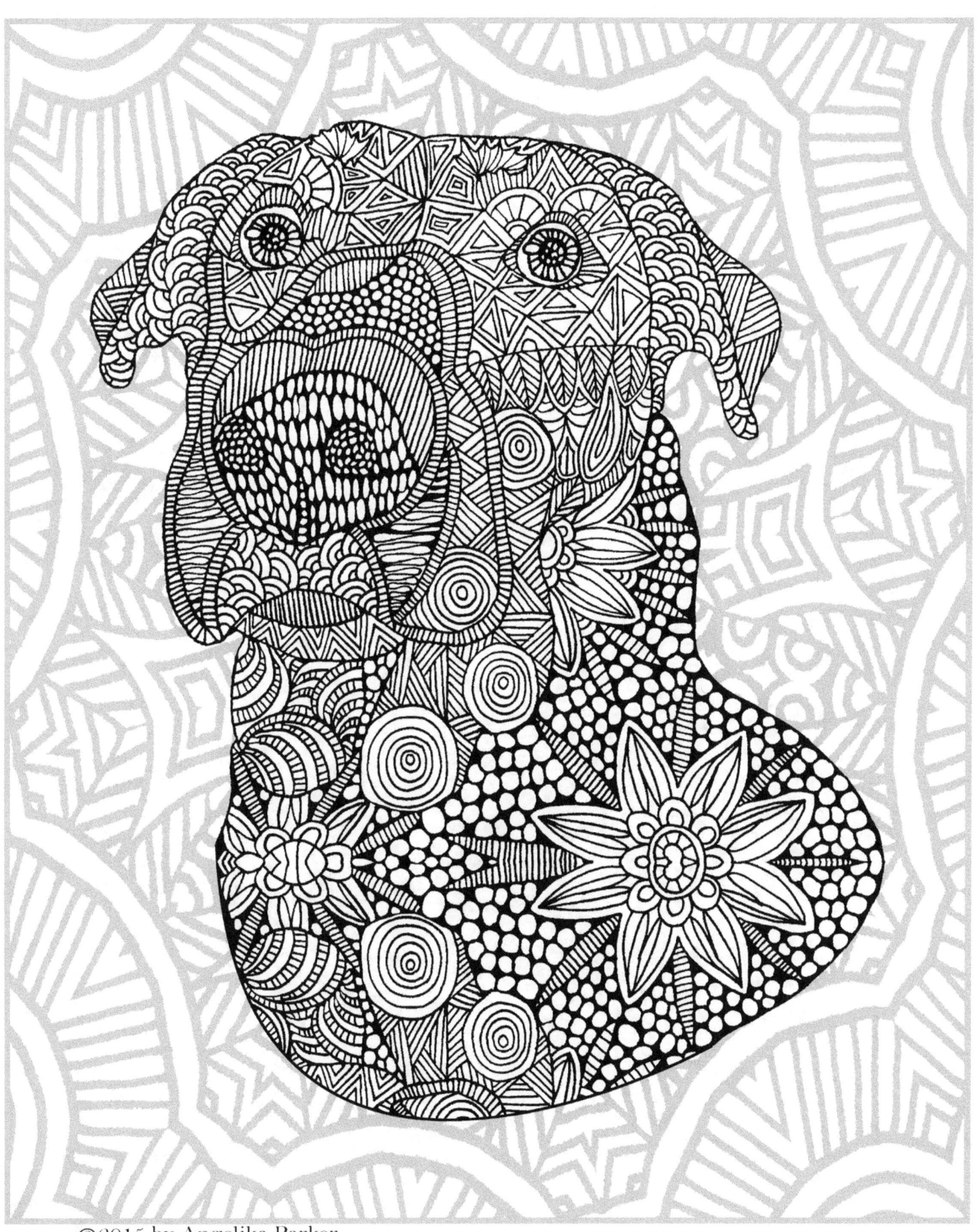

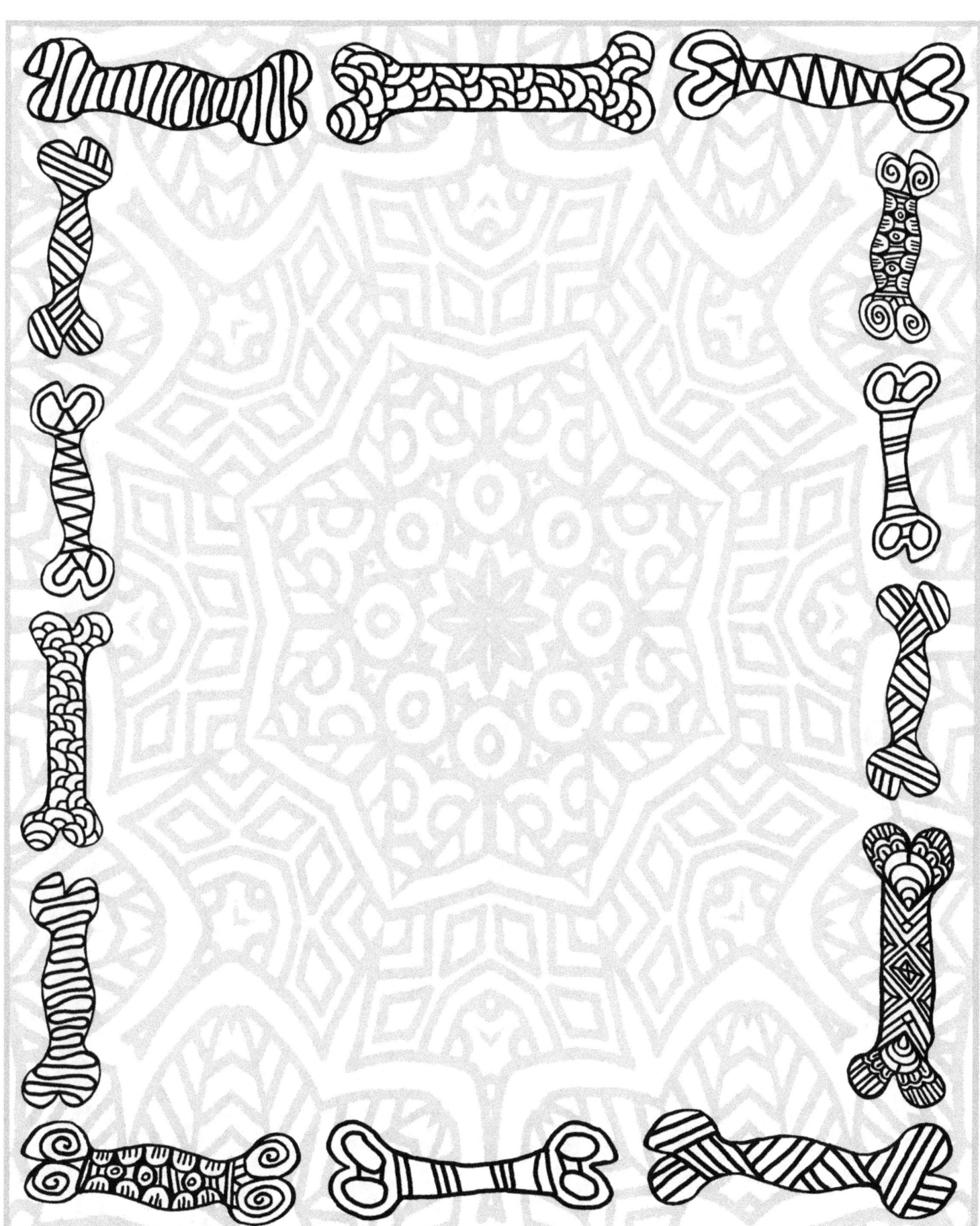

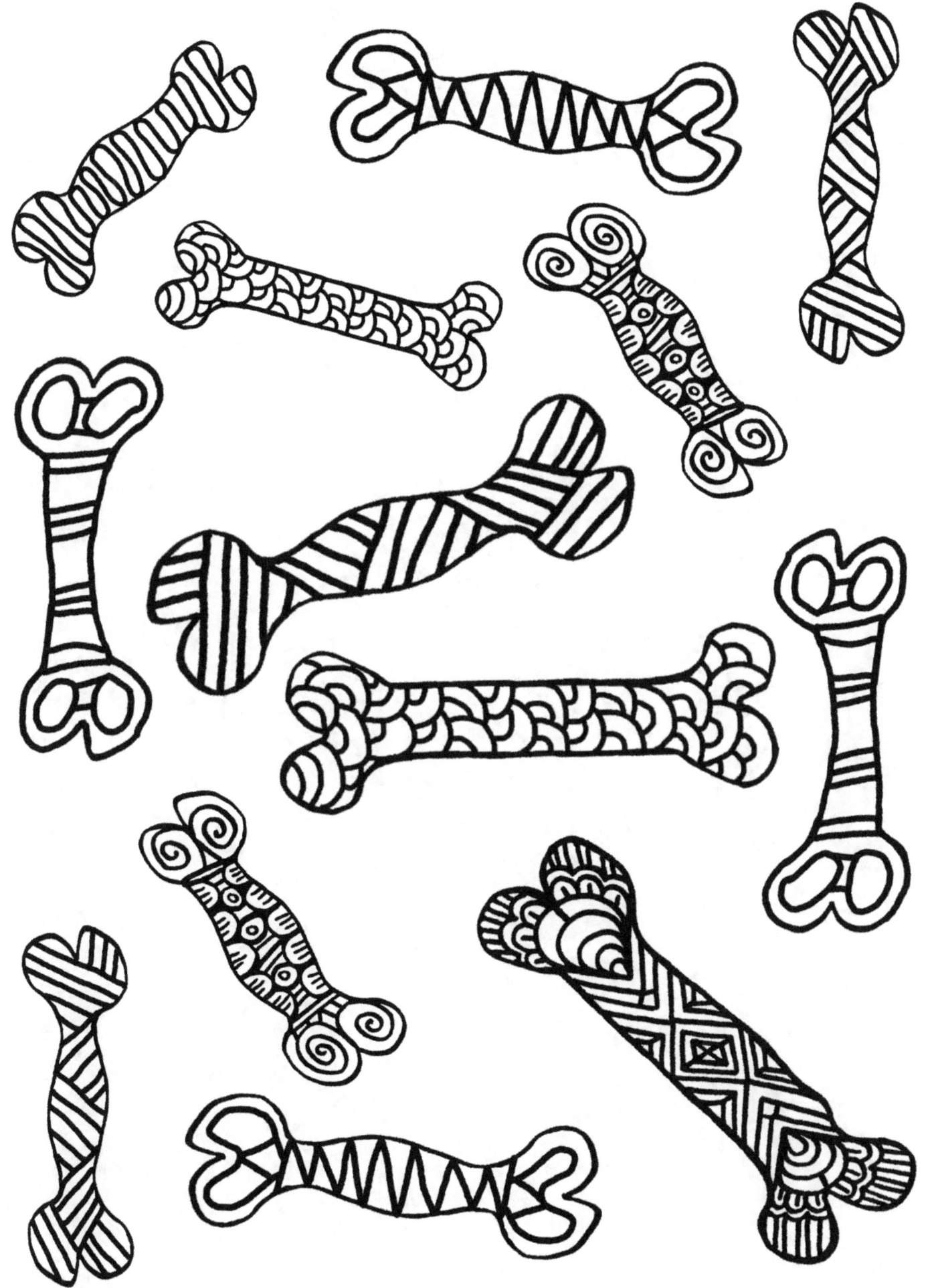

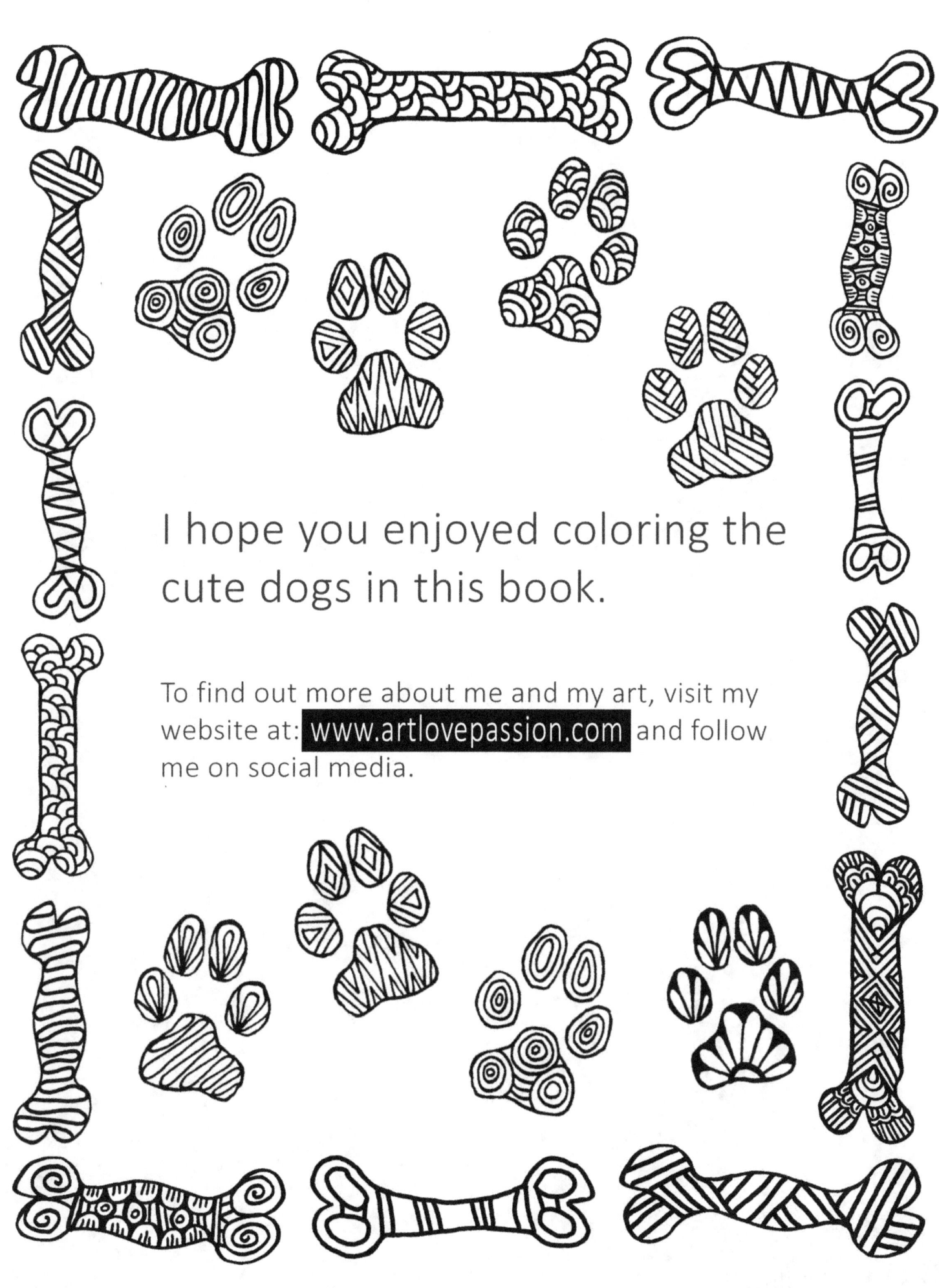

I hope you enjoyed coloring the cute dogs in this book.

To find out more about me and my art, visit my website at: www.artlovepassion.com and follow me on social media.